D1416274

Gluten-Free 101

Contributing editor: Rachel Begun, MS, RD, Rye Brook, New York

Cover photo © 2011 Brave New Pictures.
Photos on the following pages from Shutterstock: 4, 10, 13, 17, 19, 21, 26, 40, 54, 61, 68, 84, 106, 120, 132, 148.
Photos on the following pages from Brave New Pictures: 31, 47, 73, 81, 89, 101, 115, 129, 137, 153, 165.

Printed in China.

Library of Congress Cataloging-in-Publication Data

Gluten-free 101 : master gluten-free cooking with 101 great recipes / edited by Perrin Davis.

    p. cm.

Includes index.

ISBN 978-1-57284-133-8 (flexibound) -- ISBN 1-57284-133-8 (flexibound) -- ISBN 978-1-57284-701-9 (ebook) -- ISBN 1-57284-701-8 (ebook)

1. Gluten-free diet--Recipes. 2. International cooking. 3. Cookbooks. I. Davis, Perrin, 1969- II. Title: Master gluten-free cooking with 101 great recipes.

RM237.86.D38 2012

641.3--dc23

2011051912

15 14 13 12   10 9 8 7 6 5 4 3 2 1

Surrey Books is an imprint of Agate Publishing, Inc.
Agate and Surrey books are available in bulk at discount prices. For more information, go to agatepublishing.com.

Gluten-Free 101

MASTER GLUTEN-FREE COOKING WITH 101 GREAT RECIPES

EDITED BY **Perrin Davis**

S
SURREY
BOOKS

AN AGATE IMPRINT

CHICAGO

CONTENTS

INTRODUCTION

Agate Surrey Books wants to help everyone, but especially kitchen beginners, learn how to explore different kinds of food and cooking. We are proud to introduce the *101* series, which aims to provide rewarding, successful, and fun cooking experiences for everyone, from novices to more experienced cooks. *Gluten-Free 101: Master Gluten-Free Cooking with 101 Great Recipes* is one of the first books in this series, and it offers readers not only delicious recipes but also useful information about shopping for equipment, ingredients, kitchen essentials, and seasonings. Getting started with gluten-free cooking can be intimidating, but we'll demystify the process for you. So whether you or someone you love have just recently adopted a gluten-free lifestyle, or if you have been gluten-free for some time now, *Gluten-Free 101* is a great place to start.

Most of the recipes in these *101* series books come from a wide range of Agate Surrey authors and editors. Contributors to *Gluten-Free 101* include Sue Spitler, editor of the "1,001" series that includes such titles as *1,001 Best Low-Fat Recipes*; Viktorija Todorovska, author of *The Puglian Cookbook*; and Annalise Roberts and Claudia Pillow, authors of *The Gluten-Free Good Health Cookbook*.

Gluten-Free 101 recipes were selected to provide a starting point for anyone beginning their gluten-free cooking journey. The collection includes a variety of cuisines (Italian, Mexican, Southwestern, French, Middle Eastern, and Asian, to name a few). Most of the recipes are simple, although a handful of them are more advanced; you'll find that all are easy to follow.

A TASTE OF WHAT YOU'LL FIND IN THIS BOOK

This book contains lots of fantastic main-dish options in the Chicken, Meats, Fish and Seafood, and Pasta chapters. Don't miss great dinner-party options like Southwestern Braised Chuck Roast, Tandoori Lamb with Cucumber Raita, Sautéed Pork with Maple Mustard Sauce, and Chicken and Cheese Rellenos, as well

as delicious family pleasers like Chicken Parmesan and Mexican Hash. Shrimp Curry and Pasta with Chicken and Creamy Pesto Sauce will put smiles on everyone's face, and the Macaroni and Cheese is a big favorite in our house.

In the Side Dishes chapter, check out delicious dishes like Spinach and Goat Cheese Pie, Butternut Squash Gratin, Mixed Roasted Vegetables, and Egg and Broccoli Casserole.

Looking for a delightful dessert option to serve after dinner? Try the Chocolate Mousse Torte or the Hazelnut Macaroons! Chocolate Fudge Meringues, Putting on the Ritz Bars, and Bananas Foster are just a few more of the tasty offerings in the Desserts chapter. Need to delight a more sophisticated palate? Look no further than our Herbed Custard Brulée on page 161.

But before you get started cooking some of these great recipes, make sure you're up to speed on some gluten-free cooking basics, and that your kitchen and pantry are ready to go!

GLUTEN-FREE COOKING BASICS

A gluten-free lifestyle consisting of natural, wholesome foods can be very healthy. People who suffer from celiac disease cannot tolerate gluten at all, but many other people have gluten sensitivity, which leads them to feel ill after eating foods containing gluten. In addition to those with celiac disease and gluten sensitivity, some individuals with arthritis and other inflammatory or auto-immune disorders have found relief with a gluten-free diet.

A gluten-free diet consists of foods and beverages that do not include wheat in all of its many forms, including but not limited to bulgur, durum, farina, matzoh, spelt, kamut, einkorn, farro, triticale, semolina, rye, barley (including malt), and contaminated oats. While it seems that it might be simple to just avoid breads and other foods that obviously contain wheat, you may be surprised to learn that countless—in fact, many—processed foods contain gluten. Here is a list of just a few of the terms you should look for on ingredient labels that may translate to gluten-containing products:

- Alcohol (distilled alcohols are okay, but undistilled alcohol can be a problem if it is made from wheat, rye, or barley)
- Artificial color
- Beer
- Dinkle
- Emulsifiers
- Farina
- Farro
- Food starch
- Glucose syrup
- Hydrolyzed plant protein (HPP)
- Hydrolyzed protein
- Hydrolyzed vegetable protein (HVP)
- Hydrolyzed wheat gluten
- Hydrolyzed wheat protein
- Malt extract
- Malt vinegar
- Malted milk
- Modified food starch
- Natural flavoring
- Nondairy creamer
- Protein hydrolysates
- Seasonings
- Seitan
- Soy sauce
- Spelt
- Stabilizers
- Starches
- Vegetable protein
- Vegetable starch

For a more thorough list of ingredients to watch out for, check out the Unsafe Gluten-Free Food List at www.celiac.com.

A quick glance at the list will tell you one thing for sure: processed foods can be dangerous for anyone trying to avoid gluten. If you prepare foods with simple, whole ingredients, you'll know for sure whether or not your meal is gluten free. The recipes you'll find in this book are just that: simple and made with whole ingredients. In these pages, you'll find everything from pasta to tortes—many foods you thought you might not be able to enjoy again. Fortunately, there are many gluten-free products out there today, and we've included many brand recommendations to make your shopping simpler and easier. If you have a hard time finding the brands we recommend in these pages in your local grocery or specialty stores, try online options like Amazon.com. You just might find what you're looking for!

A few more tips for the smart gluten-free shopper and chef:

- Coffee is naturally gluten free, of course, but some flavored or instant coffees and espressos may contain gluten. Read the label carefully; recipes within that contain coffee or coffee powders include suggestions for gluten-free brands.

- Low-fat products, particularly dairy products, can be gluten minefields. The recipes in this book recommend full-fat dairy products, such as sour cream. Often, the fat replacers used by food manufacturers contain wheat derivatives.

- Cheese, like coffee, is naturally gluten free, but some shredded cheeses include anticaking agents that contain gluten. Buy whole cheeses and shred them yourself to make sure they're safe. The same goes for packaged shredded or cut potatoes. In the book, we recommend Simply Potatoes as a brand that is gluten free.

- Broths may contain gluten as well. All Pacific Natural Foods broths—except its Organic Mushroom Broth—are gluten free. And of course, if you make your broth yourself, you'll know it's gluten free.

KITCHEN EQUIPMENT BASICS

If you are a new cook, or it's been a while since you've spent time in the kitchen, here is some helpful information that will make it easy to jump into *Gluten-Free 101* recipes. The following is not necessarily gluten-free–cooking specific, but if you have the following equipment, you will be prepared to make almost any recipe in this book.

Appliances

We're sure you know this already, but your kitchen should include the following standard set of appliances.

Pretty Much Mandatory

- Refrigerator/freezer (set to about 34°F to 38°F [1°C to 3°C], or as cold as you can get it without freezing vegetables or drinks)

- Freezer (if yours is not frost-free, you'll periodically need to unplug it to defrost your snow-filled box)

- Stove/oven (make sure to keep the oven very clean, as burnt foods and other odors can affect the taste of your food)

- Microwave (again, make sure it's clean and ready for use), because it's great for defrosting

- Blender (and not just for beverages and soups—you can use it in place of a food processor or an immersion blender in some instances)

- Hand mixer (you can always stir by hand, but sometimes, the hand mixer is indispensable)

Optional

- Food processor
- Immersion blender

- Stand mixer
- Slow cooker

Pots and Pans

The following are useful basic equipment for any kitchen.

- Stockpot (8 to 10 quarts [7.6 to 9.5 L])
- Dutch oven (5 to 6 quarts [4.7 to 5.7 L])
- Pancake griddle
- Large stockpot with lid (6 to 8 quarts [5.7 to 7.6 L])
- Large skillet with lid (10 to 12 inches in diameter [25 to 30 cm])
- Medium skillet with lid (7 to 8 inches in diameter [17.5 to 20 cm])
- Medium and large saucepans with lids (2 and 3 quarts [1.9 to 2.8 L])
- Small saucepan with lid (1 quart [.95 L])
- Glass casserole dish (2 quarts [1.9 L])
- Square cake pan (8 or 9 inches [20 to 22.5 cm])
- Rectangular cake pan (13 by 9 inches [32.5 by 22.5 cm])
- 2 loaf pans (8 inches [20 cm] long)
- Muffin pan (12 muffins)
- Pie pan (9 inches in diameter [22.5 cm])
- 2 baking sheets

General Utensils

The following are recommended basics for any kitchen.

- Knives: Chef's knife, serrated knife, and paring knife
- Measuring cups for both dry and liquid measures
- Measuring spoons
- Mixing bowls (two or three, ranging from 1 or 2 quarts to 5 or 6 quarts [.95 or 1.9 L to 4.7 or 5.7 L])
- Wooden spoons, slotted spoon, rubber or silicone spatula, ladle, whisk, tongs, and a large metal "flipper" for burgers and similar foods
- Colander
- Cheese grater
- Citrus zester
- Salt and pepper mills
- Kitchen scissors
- Vegetable peeler
- Can opener
- Cooling rack
- Kitchen timer
- Cutting boards
- Pot holders
- Kitchen towels

Storage and Paper Supplies

Either in a handy drawer or on a shelf, make sure you have all of these items within easy reach.

- Plastic or glass storage containers (5 to 10, varying sizes)
- Aluminum foil
- Plastic wrap
- Parchment paper
- Small zip-top bags
- Large zip-top bags
- Muffin cup liners

BASIC INGREDIENTS LIST FOR GLUTEN-FREE COOKING

This section includes the basics that you should have on hand, but this is by no means a comprehensive list for every recipe in this book. If you have these ingredients as a starting point, however, you'll be in great shape to tackle almost any of the *Gluten-Free 101* recipes!

Seasonings and Flavorings

A note about spices: Single-ingredient dried herbs and spices are always gluten-free, but beware mixed or blended spices (like curry or Chinese five-spice powder) or powders (garlic, onion, etc.), as they sometimes contain flour or other gluten-containing products. Read every label very carefully. The spice company McCormick is committed to including clear mention of any gluten-containing ingredients directly on its labels.

- Bay leaves
- Cayenne pepper
- Chili powder (make sure you select a gluten-free brand, as chili powders are blended)
- Curry powder (make sure you select a gluten-free brand, as curry powders are blended)
- Ground cumin
- Dry mustard
- Garlic powder (make sure you select a gluten-free brand, as garlic powders may contain additives)
- Ground cinnamon
- Ground ginger
- Ground nutmeg
- Red pepper flakes
- Rosemary
- Italian seasoning (make sure you select a gluten-free brand, as Italian seasoning is blended)
- Oregano
- Paprika
- Kosher salt
- Vanilla extract (all McCormick's extracts are gluten free)
- White pepper

- Freshly ground black pepper
- Chicken, beef, and vegetable base (just add water to them to make instant broth—make sure you select a gluten-free brand, like Better than Bouillon's kosher varieties of chicken and vegetable bases)

Condiments

A note about vinegars: Most vinegars that are made in the U.S. are made from wine, corn, or potatoes—and thus, they are gluten free. The exception is malt vinegar, which should always be avoided. All distilled vinegars are fine, but do make sure to avoid undistilled vinegars, as they may contain gluten. As always, carefully read labels.

- Apple cider vinegar
- Balsamic vinegar
- Red wine vinegar
- Rice vinegar
- White wine vinegar
- Honey
- Hot pepper sauce (Frank's RedHot Original is gluten free)
- Ketchup (I recommend Heinz)
- Mustard (French's is gluten free)
- Olive oil
- Gluten-free soy sauce (San-J is excellent)
- Vegetable oil
- Worcestershire sauce (Lea & Perrins is gluten free)

Baking

- Corn starch
- Baking powder (Clabber Girl is gluten free)
- Baking soda (Arm & Hammer is gluten free)
- Butter (margarine can be tricky—it sometimes contains gluten; stay on the safe side and stick with butter)
- Vegetable shortening (Spectrum organic shortening is gluten free)

- 2% milk
- Pure maple syrup
- Pure molasses
- Granulated sugar
- Light brown sugar
- Brown rice flour (Bob's Red Mill is an excellent source)
- Cocoa powder (Ghirardelli Unsweetened is a good choice)
- Fresh large eggs

General

- Brown rice
- Garlic
- Gluten-free pasta (I recommend Glutino and Schar brands)
- Onions
- Canned tomatoes (Muir Glen's organic fire-roasted and regular tomatoes are truly delicious and gluten free)
- Lentils
- Raisins
- Tomato sauce (Muir Glen is gluten free)

- Chicken, beef, and vegetable broth and stock (all Pacific Natural Foods broths—except its Organic Mushroom Broth—are gluten free; Swanson Natural Goodness Beef Stock is a great gluten-free beef stock choice)

- All of the recipes in this book call for fresh cuts of meat, poultry, or fish and seafood. Always avoid preseasoned or packaged meats or fish, because you can't be sure about what ingredients they contain.

COMMON COOKING TERMS

You probably are quite familiar with most of these terms. If this is your first time cooking or it's been a while since you've been in the kitchen, here is a quick refresher:

- **Brown:** To cook a meat at a high temperature for a very brief period of time in order to seal in the juices and add a tremendous amount of flavor. You'll see this in a lot of this book's recipes, because it's a great flavor booster. Browning should take no more than 2 or 3 minutes on each side and is done before thoroughly cooking the meat. It may be tempting to skip this step, but please don't…it's really worth the few minutes in terms of the flavor and texture of the meat once your recipe is complete.

- **Bake:** To cook food with dry heat, usually in the oven at a specified temperature.

- **Boil:** To cook food in boiling water (212°F [100°C]) on the stovetop.

- **Blanch:** A technique that involves immersing food in boiling water for a brief period of time and then immediately transferring into an ice bath in order to stop the cooking process. Blanching is an excellent technique for quickly cooking tender vegetables, as it helps them retain their firmness, crispness, and color.

- **Braise:** This technique is a combination of browning the surface of meat, which means to cook at a high temperature for a short amount of time, followed by cooking at a lower temperature in a covered pot with liquid for a longer period of time.

- **Broil:** To cook over a high heat at a specified distance from the heat source, usually in the oven or in the "broiler" part of the oven.

- **Deep fry:** To cook food by immersing it in preheated oil.

- **Grill:** To cook over an open flame on a metal framework, grid, or other cooking surface.

- **Roast:** To cook meat in an oven in an uncovered dish, usually resulting in a well-browned surface that seals in juices and flavors.

- **Sauté:** To cook food over a medium-high or high heat in a skillet or sauté pan in a small amount of oil, water, stock, or other liquid.

- **Steam:** To cook food with steam, usually in a steamer rack or basket positioned over (but not immersed in) a pan containing a small amount of water.

- **Stir-fry:** To cook over high heat with a small amount of oil; usually requires regular stirring as food is cooking. It can be used for several kinds of dishes and is often associated with Asian fare.

GENERAL COOKING TIPS

No matter what you're cooking or how many people you're serving, a few universal rules of the kitchen will make your life easier. The following is a list of our recommendations for the novice cook. These great habits will ensure fewer mistakes, less stress, and ultimately more delicious food.

- **Read every recipe from beginning to end, at least twice, before you start cooking.** This will help to ensure that you understand how it should be made and what you need to make it.

- **Set up your ingredients, pots, pans, and utensils before you begin to prepare the recipes.** We never start a recipe until we have every ingredient on the counter in front of us. (If possible, we also premeasure all the ingredients and have them ready to add, because there's nothing worse than accidentally dumping half a box of kosher salt into an almost-finished recipe.) If you know you'll need a greased pan in step 4, grease it and set it aside before you even get started.

- **Keep a grocery list and a pen attached to the refrigerator.** If you go to the grocery store without a specific list of what you need, you're likely to forget at least a few items.

- **Clean up as you go.** If you take the time to clean your dishes as you're cooking, you'll find that you will have more space to work in and less to do after the meal is done.

- **Time the meal.** It can be complicated to cook multiple recipes at once and make sure that everything ends up finishing at roughly the same time. Make sure you allow for enough time for everything to get done, and for recipes to be cooked simultaneously.

- **Be careful.** It sounds silly, but never forget that you're working with high-temperature appliances and cookware and sharp utensils! Use proper precaution when lifting lids, turning pans, and straining vegetables.

- **Have fun!** We hope you enjoy learning how to cook these recipes and sharing them with others.

APPETIZERS AND SNACKS

BEANS AND GREENS

This dish is easy to make, yet full of flavor and deeply satisfying. I often serve it as an appetizer to kick off a dinner party. This recipe comes from The Puglian Cookbook *by Viktorija Todorovska.*

8 SERVINGS

FOR THE BEAN SPREAD:

2 cups (368 g) dried chickpeas
1 large yellow onion, cut into quarters
1 large carrot, peeled and cut into 1-inch (2.5-cm) pieces
3 cloves garlic, whole
2 teaspoons sea salt, plus more, to taste

1. Soak the beans overnight in cold water.

2. Drain the beans and put them in a large pot. Add water to cover the beans by about 2 inches (5 cm). Add the onion, carrot, garlic, and about 2 teaspoons salt, and bring to a boil.

3. Reduce the heat to low and cook slowly for about 3 hours, until the beans are soft and can be mashed with a wooden spoon.

4. Drain, reserving 1 cup (236 mL) of the cooking liquid. When the beans are cool enough to handle, remove the onion and carrot.

5. Put the beans and garlic in a food processor and pulse until the purée reaches a uniform consistency. If the purée is too dry, gradually add a little of the cooking water. Add salt to taste.

FOR THE GREENS:

2 bunches dandelion greens, washed and cut into bite-sized pieces

Salt, to taste

Olive oil, for drizzling

Dippers: fresh vegetables, sliced

1. In a medium pot, bring 2 quarts (1.9 L) of water to a boil. Add the greens and salt and cook for 2 to 3 minutes, until the greens are wilted. Drain immediately.

2. Serve the beans surrounded by the greens. Drizzle the dish with the olive oil, and use the fresh vegetables to scoop the spread.

SAUSAGE AND EGG PIZZA >

Try this delightful appetizer at your next party!

- 2 large poblano chilies, sliced
- 1 cup (150 g) chopped onion
- 1 clove garlic, minced
- 8 eggs, lightly beaten
- ¼ cup (59 mL) 2% milk
- 4 ounces (114 g) Italian-style sausage, cooked, crumbled (be sure to select a gluten-free brand, such as Applegate Farms)
- Salt and pepper, to taste
- Potato Pizza Crust (recipe follows)
- ½–1 cup (57–114 g) shredded mozzarella cheese (shred your own to ensure no wheat products are added to prevent caking)

1. Cook the chilies, onion, and garlic in a lightly greased large skillet over medium to medium-low heat until the chilies are very soft, for 20 to 30 minutes. Remove from the skillet.

2. Add the combined eggs and milk to the skillet; cook until eggs are just set, stirring occasionally. Stir in the sausage and chili mixture; season to taste with the salt and pepper.

3. Spoon the mixture onto the prepared Potato Pizza Crust and sprinkle with the cheese; bake at 400°F (200°C) until the cheese is melted, for about 5 minutes. Serve immediately.

POTATO PIZZA CRUST

1 CRUST

1 package (1¼ pounds [568 g]) refrigerated shredded potatoes for hash browns (Simply Potatoes is gluten free)
⅓ cup (50 g) finely chopped onion
1 egg
¼ teaspoon salt
¼ teaspoon pepper
Vegetable cooking spray

1. Mix all ingredients, except vegetable cooking spray; press mixture evenly on bottom and 1 inch up side of lightly greased 12 inch (30 cm) ovenproof skillet. Spray potatoes with cooking spray. Bake at 400°F (200°C) until browned, for about 20 minutes.

Note: Make the Potato Pizza Crust while preparing the rest of the recipe.

POTATO FRITTATA

This is the perfect light appetizer, especially for vegetarians. In Italy, frittata is served as an appetizer at room temperature, so making it ahead of time will allow you to enjoy the company of your guests.

4 SERVINGS

3 medium Yukon Gold potatoes, peeled and cubed

5 tablespoons (75 mL) extra virgin olive oil, divided

1 medium onion, peeled and chopped

½ cup (50 g) grated pecorino cheese (a sheep's milk cheese similar to Parmigiano-Reggiano; grate your own to ensure no wheat products are added to prevent caking)

½ cup (15 g) chopped parsley

6 large eggs

6–10 tablespoons (90–150 mL) 2% milk

Salt, to taste

Freshly ground black pepper, to taste

1. Preheat the oven to 400°F (200°C).

2. Boil the potatoes in salted water until done (a fork should go through the potato cubes with little effort). Drain the potatoes and set aside.

3. In a pan, heat 2 tablespoons of the olive oil. Add the onion and cook until it is soft and translucent.

4. In a large bowl, combine the cooked potatoes, cooked onions, pecorino cheese, and parsley.

5. In a separate bowl, beat together the eggs and milk for about 30 seconds, or until combined. Add the egg and milk mixture to the potato mixture and stir to combine. The mixture should be quite liquid. If it is thick, add more milk. Season with the salt and pepper.

6. Pour the remaining olive oil in a large, oven-safe pan and swirl it around to cover the bottom and sides. Pour the egg mixture into the pan and cook in the oven for 15 minutes, or until the eggs are set. Brown the frittata under the broiler for a couple of minutes. Serve hot or at room temperature.

ROASTED GARLIC AND THREE-CHEESE SPREAD

For best flavor, make this dip a day in advance.

12 SERVINGS (ABOUT 2 TABLESPOONS EACH)

1 small bulb garlic

Olive oil cooking spray

8 ounces (227 g) Neufchâtel or cream cheese, room temperature

1½–2 ounces (42–57 g) goat cheese

¼ cup (25 g) grated Parmesan cheese (grate your own to ensure no wheat products are added to prevent caking)

⅛ teaspoon white pepper

2–4 tablespoons 2% milk

Dippers: fresh vegetables, sliced

1. Cut off the top of the garlic bulb to expose the cloves. Spray the garlic lightly with cooking spray and wrap in aluminum foil; bake at 400°F (200°C) until very tender, for 35 to 40 minutes. Cool; gently press the cloves to remove them from the skins. Mash the cloves with a fork.

2. Mix the cheeses, garlic, and white pepper in a bowl, adding enough milk to make desired spreading consistency. Refrigerate for 2 to 3 hours for the flavors to blend. Serve with the fresh vegetables.

SUN-DRIED TOMATO HUMMUS

Sun-dried tomatoes and herbs embellish this Mediterranean favorite.

8 SERVINGS (ABOUT ¼ CUP [59 ML] EACH)

1 can (15 ounces [426 g]) chickpeas (garbanzo beans), rinsed, drained

⅓ cup (79 mL) plain Greek yogurt (Chobani is gluten free)

2–3 tablespoons (30–45 mL) tahini (sesame seed paste)

3 cloves garlic

4 sun-dried tomato halves (not packed in oil), finely chopped

1 teaspoon dried oregano

1 teaspoon mint leaves

2–3 teaspoons lemon juice

Salt and white pepper, to taste

Dippers: fresh vegetables, sliced

1. Process the chickpeas (garbanzo beans), yogurt, tahini, and garlic in a food processor until smooth. Stir in the sun-dried tomatoes, oregano, and mint; season to taste with the lemon juice, salt, and white pepper. Refrigerate for 1 to 2 hours so the flavors can blend. Serve with the fresh vegetables.

BAKED ARTICHOKE DIP

Everyone's favorite!

1 can (15 ounces [426 g]) artichoke hearts, rinsed, drained

½ package (8-ounce [227-g] size) Neufchâtel or cream cheese, softened

½ cup (45 g) grated Parmesan cheese (grate your own to ensure no wheat products are added to prevent caking)

½ cup (119 mL) mayonnaise

½ cup (119 mL) sour cream (beware low-fat varieties, as they may contain food starches—check labels carefully)

1–2 teaspoons lemon juice

1 green onion, thinly sliced

2 teaspoons minced garlic

2–3 drops red pepper sauce

Salt and cayenne pepper, to taste

Dippers: fresh vegetables, sliced

1. Process the artichoke hearts, cream cheese, Parmesan cheese, mayonnaise, sour cream, and lemon juice in a food processor until smooth. Stir in the green onion, garlic, and red pepper sauce. Season to taste with the salt and cayenne pepper.

2. Bake in a small casserole, uncovered, at 350°F (180°C) until lightly browned, for 20 to 25 minutes. Serve warm with the fresh vegetables.

EGGPLANT CAVIAR

Middle Eastern flavors will tempt you to second helpings! This recipe comes from 1,001 Best Low-Fat Recipes by Sue Spitler.

6 SERVINGS (ABOUT 2 TABLESPOONS EACH)

1 large eggplant (1½ pounds [681 g])
½ (80 g) cup chopped tomato
¼ (38 g) cup finely chopped onion
3 cloves garlic, minced
¼ cup (59 mL) plain Greek yogurt (Chobani is gluten free)
2 teaspoons extra-virgin olive oil
½ teaspoon dried oregano leaves
1–2 tablespoons lemon juice
Salt and pepper, to taste
4 pitted ripe olives, chopped
Dippers: fresh vegetables, sliced

1. Pierce the eggplant in several places with the fork; place in a baking pan. Bake at 350°F (180°C) until the eggplant is soft, for 45 to 50 minutes; cool. Cut the eggplant in half; scoop out the pulp with a spoon. Mash the eggplant and mix with the tomato, onion, garlic, yogurt, olive oil, and oregano in a bowl; season to taste with the lemon juice, salt, and pepper. Garnish with the olives. Refrigerate for 3 to 4 hours so the flavors can blend. Serve with the fresh vegetables.

PINE NUT SPINACH PÂTÉ

Toasted pine nuts provide flavor and texture accents in this unique dip.

12 SERVINGS (ABOUT 2 TABLESPOONS EACH)

1 package (10 ounces [284 g]) frozen chopped spinach, thawed, well drained

¼ cup (38 g) coarsely chopped onion

¼ cup (38 g) celery

1 clove garlic

2–3 teaspoons lemon juice

1 teaspoon dried dill weed

1–2 tablespoons toasted pine nuts or slivered almonds

4 ounces (114 g) Neufchâtel or cream cheese, room temperature

Salt and pepper, to taste

Dippers: fresh vegetables, sliced

1. Process the spinach, onion, celery, garlic, lemon juice, and dill weed in the food processor until almost smooth; add the pine nuts and process until coarsely chopped. Stir in the cream cheese; season to taste with the salt and pepper. Refrigerate for several hours so the flavors can blend. Serve with the fresh vegetables.

WILD MUSHROOM PÂTÉ

This pâté is most flavorful when made with wild mushrooms, though any type of mushrooms can be used.

8 SERVINGS (ABOUT 2 TABLESPOONS EACH)

12 ounces (341 g) coarsely chopped shiitake or portobello mushrooms

½ cup (75 g) chopped onion

2–4 cloves garlic, minced

¼ cup (59 mL) dry sherry or water

2 tablespoons grated Parmesan cheese (grate your own to ensure no wheat products are added to prevent caking)

2–3 teaspoons lemon juice

Salt and pepper, to taste

Dippers: fresh vegetables, sliced

1. Cook the mushrooms, onion, garlic, and sherry in a lightly greased skillet, covered, over medium heat until the mushrooms are wilted, for about 5 minutes. Cook, uncovered, over medium heat until the vegetables are very tender and all the liquid is gone, for 8 to 10 minutes. Cool.

2. Process the mushroom mixture and the Parmesan cheese in a food processor until smooth. Season to taste with the lemon juice, salt, and pepper. Refrigerate for 2 to 3 hours so the flavors can blend. Serve in a crock with the fresh vegetables.

SOUPS AND STEWS

FLORIDA AVOCADO AND TOMATO CHOWDER

In this easy recipe, colorful ingredients create a kaleidoscope of fresh flavors.

4 SERVINGS (ABOUT 1½ CUPS [356 ML] EACH)

- 3 cups (450 g) cubed, peeled potatoes
- 1 can (14 ounces [420 mL]) chicken broth (Pacific Natural Foods chicken broth is gluten free)
- 1 teaspoon dried thyme leaves
- 8 ounces (227 g) smoked turkey breast, cubed (Boar's Head's entire line of meats and cheeses is gluten free)
- 1 cup (160 g) whole kernel corn
- 1 cup (160 g) chopped plum tomatoes
- 1 cup (150 g) cubed avocado
- Juice of 1 lime
- 3 slices bacon, cooked, crumbled (Hormel's Black Label brand is gluten free)
- Salt and pepper, to taste

1. Heat the potatoes, broth, and thyme to boiling in a medium saucepan; reduce the heat and simmer, covered, until the potatoes are tender, for about 10 minutes. Using a slotted spoon, transfer ½ of the potatoes to a medium bowl. Process the remaining mixture in a food processor or blender until smooth; return to the saucepan. Add the turkey, corn, and reserved potatoes; heat to boiling. Reduce the heat and simmer 5 minutes. Stir in the tomatoes, avocado, lime juice, and bacon. Season to taste with the salt and pepper. Serve immediately.

SHIITAKE–PORTOBELLO CHOWDER

Celebrate the rich mushroom, cheese, and wine flavors in this chowder.

4 SERVINGS (ABOUT 1½ CUPS [356 ML] EACH)

4 shallots, thinly sliced

2 teaspoons butter, divided

2 large potatoes, cubed (¼-inch [6 mm])

3 cups (711 mL) chicken broth (Pacific Natural Foods chicken broth is gluten free)

2 cups (150 g) sliced shiitake mushroom caps

2 cups (150 g) cubed portobello mushrooms

¼ cup (28 g) shredded Gruyère or Swiss cheese (shred your own to ensure no wheat products are added to prevent caking)

2 tablespoons Marsala wine (optional)

Salt and white pepper, to taste

1. Sauté the shallots in 1 teaspoon of the butter in a large saucepan for 2 to 3 minutes; add the potatoes and broth and heat to boiling. Reduce the heat and simmer, covered, until the potatoes are tender, for about 15 minutes. Process the mixture in a blender or food processor until smooth; return to the saucepan.

2. Sauté the mushrooms in the remaining 1 teaspoon of butter in a large skillet until lightly browned, for about 8 minutes; stir into the potato mixture. Cook, uncovered, over medium heat until hot, for about 5 minutes. Remove from the heat; add the cheese and wine, stirring until cheese is melted. Season to taste with the salt and white pepper. Serve immediately.

CINNAMON-SPICED PUMPKIN SOUP

For convenience, 2 cans (16 ounces [454 g] each) of pumpkin can be substituted for the fresh pumpkin. Any yellow winter squash, such as butternut, Hubbard, or acorn, can also be used. This recipe comes from 1,001 Best Low-Fat Recipes by Sue Spitler.

4 SERVINGS (ABOUT 1¼ CUPS [296 ML] EACH)

4 cups (464 g) cubed, seeded, peeled pumpkin

2 cups (474 mL) half-and-half or 2% milk

1–2 tablespoons light brown sugar

½ teaspoon ground cinnamon

¼–½ teaspoon ground nutmeg

Snipped chives, as garnish

1. Cook the pumpkin in a medium saucepan, covered, in 1 inch (2.5 cm) of simmering water until tender, for about 15 minutes; drain. Process the pumpkin and half-and-half in a food processor or blender; return to the saucepan. Stir in the brown sugar and spices and heat to boiling; reduce the heat and simmer, uncovered, for 5 minutes. Sprinkle each bowl of soup with the chives. Serve immediately.

INDIAN LENTIL SOUP

This soup (dal shorba), which hails from India, is flavored with curry powder and sweet coriander. Red, green, or brown lentils can be used.

8 SERVINGS (ABOUT 1 CUP [237 ML] EACH)

½ cup (75 g) chopped onion

1 clove garlic, minced

2 teaspoons curry powder (I prefer McCormick's spices, because they always list flour on the ingredient label if it's included—check the label carefully to ensure your curry powder is gluten free)

1 teaspoon crushed coriander seeds

1 teaspoon crushed cumin seeds

½ teaspoon ground turmeric

¼ teaspoon crushed red pepper flakes

1 tablespoon olive oil

5 cups (1.9 L) chicken broth (Pacific Natural Foods chicken broth is gluten free)

4 cups (948 mL) water

2 cups (384 g) dried red or brown lentils

Salt and pepper, to taste

6 tablespoons (90 mL) plain Greek yogurt (Chobani is gluten free)

1. Sauté the onion, garlic, curry powder, herbs, and red pepper in the oil in a large saucepan until the onion is tender, for about 5 minutes. Add the broth, water, and lentils; heat to boiling. Reduce the heat and simmer, covered, until the lentils are tender, for about 30 minutes. Season to taste with the salt and pepper. Top each bowl of soup with a tablespoon of yogurt. Serve immediately.

PAPRIKA-SIRLOIN STEW WITH SOUR CREAM >

Tender beef and vegetables in a paprika-spiked sour cream sauce are ready to eat in less than 45 minutes.

4 SERVINGS

1 pound boneless beef sirloin steak, fat trimmed, cut into strips (1 x ½-inch [2.5 x 1.3 cm])

1 cup (150 g) pearl onions, peeled

1 cup (237 mL) beef broth or stock (Swanson's Beef Stock is gluten free)

2 cups (300 g) Italian green beans

¾ pound (341 g) red potatoes, cubed

1 can (15 ounces [426 g]) diced tomatoes (I use Muir Glen diced tomatoes), undrained

2 bay leaves

1 tablespoon paprika

½ cup (119 mL) sour cream (beware low-fat varieties, as they may contain food starches—check labels carefully)

Salt and pepper, to taste

1. Sauté the beef and onions in a lightly greased large skillet until lightly browned, for 8 to 10 minutes; add the remaining ingredients, except the sour cream, salt, and pepper, and heat to boiling. Reduce the heat and simmer until the beef and vegetables are tender, for about 15 minutes. Stir in the sour cream; season to taste with the salt and pepper. Serve immediately.

SHRIMP AND BLACK BEAN SOUP

In Mexico, leaves from the avocado tree are used for seasoning in this favorite Oaxacan soup. We've substituted a bay leaf, which is somewhat stronger in flavor.

6 SERVINGS (ABOUT 1½ CUPS [356 ML] EACH)

2 medium onions, chopped

4 cloves garlic, minced

2 medium tomatoes, cut into wedges

3 cans (14½ ounces [435 mL] each) chicken broth (Pacific Natural Foods chicken broth is gluten free), divided

½ cup (119 mL) water

3 cups (516 g) cooked dried black beans or 2 cans (15 ounces [426 g] each) black beans, rinsed, drained

1 teaspoon dried oregano leaves

1 teaspoon dried thyme leaves

1 teaspoon ground cumin

1 bay leaf

8 ounces (227 g) peeled, deveined shrimp

Salt and pepper, to taste

Finely chopped cilantro, as garnish

1. Sauté the onions and garlic in a lightly greased medium saucepan until tender, for about 5 minutes. Process the onion mixture, tomatoes, and 1 can of the chicken broth in a food processor or blender until smooth; return to the saucepan. Add the remaining 2 cans of broth, the water, the beans, and herbs; heat to boiling. Reduce the heat and simmer, uncovered, for 10 minutes, adding the shrimp during the last 5 minutes. Discard the bay leaf. Season to taste with the salt and pepper; sprinkle with the cilantro. Serve immediately.

GREEK BEEF AND LENTIL STEW

Lentils and fresh vegetables partner deliciously in this easy stew.

6 SERVINGS (ABOUT 1½ CUPS [356 ML] EACH)

1 cup (150 g) chopped onion

1 cup (150 g) green bell pepper

1 cup (124 g) cubed zucchini

2 teaspoons minced garlic

2 cups (300 g) cubed Idaho potatoes

2 cups (300 g) cut green beans

1 cup (192 g) lentils

1 can (15 ounces [426 g]) diced tomatoes, undrained (Muir Glen's organic fire-roasted diced tomatoes are truly delicious and gluten free)

3 cups beef broth or stock (Swanson's Beef Stock is gluten free)

1 teaspoon dried oregano leaves

1 teaspoon dried mint leaves

½ teaspoon ground turmeric

½ teaspoon ground coriander

12 ounces (341 g) cooked, cubed beef eye of round

Salt and pepper, to taste

1. Sauté the onion, bell pepper, zucchini, and garlic in a lightly greased large saucepan until tender, for about 5 minutes. Add the remaining ingredients, except the salt and pepper; heat to boiling. Reduce the heat and simmer, covered, until the lentils are just tender and the stew is thickened, for 20 to 30 minutes. Season to taste with the salt and pepper. Serve immediately.

CARIBBEAN GINGER BEAN AND PORK STEW

Fresh gingerroot accents the flavor contrasts in this colorful stew.

6 SERVINGS

12 ounces (341 g) boneless pork loin, fat trimmed, cubed
(¾-inch [1.9-cm])
1 tablespoon olive oil, chopped gingerroot
1 cup (150 g) chopped onion
2 teaspoons minced garlic
2 teaspoons jalapeño chili
1 can (15 ounces [426 g]) black beans, rinsed, drained
1 can (15 ounces [426 g]) black-eyed peas, rinsed, drained
¾ cup (113 g) fresh or frozen cut okra
1 cup (237 mL) orange juice
1 cup (320 g) jalapeño chili jelly (Baxters is gluten free) or
orange marmalade (Bonne Maman is gluten free)
½ teaspoon dried thyme leaves
1 can (11 ounces [312 g]) mandarin orange segments,
drained
Salt and pepper, to taste
3 cups (570 g) cooked brown or white rice

1. Sauté the pork in the oil in a large skillet until browned, for 5 to 8 minutes. Add the gingerroot, onion, bell pepper, garlic, and jalapeño chili and sauté until tender, for about 5 minutes. Add the black beans, black-eyed peas, okra, orange juice, jelly, and thyme; heat to boiling. Reduce the heat and simmer, covered, until the okra is tender, for about 10 minutes. Add the orange segments; cook for 1 to 2 minutes. Season to taste with the salt and pepper; serve immediately over the rice.

ROSEMARY LAMB STEW WITH SWEET POTATOES

The pairing of rosemary and lamb is classic, distinctive, and delightful.

4 SERVINGS

> 1 pound (454 g) boneless lamb shoulder, fat trimmed, cubed (¾-inch [1.9-cm])
>
> 1 teaspoon olive oil
>
> 1 large onion, cut into thin wedges
>
> 2 tablespoons chopped fresh or 1 teaspoon dried rosemary leaves
>
> 3 cups (711 mL) beef broth or stock (Swanson's Beef Stock is gluten free)
>
> 2 bay leaves
>
> 1¼ pounds (568 g) sweet potatoes, freshly peeled and cubed (¾-inch [1.9-cm])
>
> 1½ cups (225 g) cut green beans
>
> Salt and pepper, to taste

1. Sauté the lamb in oil in a large saucepan until lightly browned, for about 8 minutes. Add the onion and rosemary; sauté 5 minutes. Add the broth and bay leaves; heat to boiling. Reduce the heat and simmer, covered, until the lamb is tender, for 1 to 1½ hours, adding the sweet potatoes and green beans during the last 15 minutes. Discard the bay leaves; season to taste with the salt and pepper. Serve immediately.

GINGER-ORANGE CHICKEN AND SQUASH STEW

Any winter squash, such as acorn, butternut, or Hubbard, is appropriate for this orange and ginger accented stew; sweet potatoes can be used too.

6 SERVINGS

1 pound (454 g) boneless, skinless chicken breast, cubed

1 cup (150 g) coarsely chopped onions

1 cup (150 g) green bell peppers

2 cloves garlic, minced

1 tablespoon olive oil

3 cups (372 g) cubed, peeled winter yellow squash

2 medium Idaho potatoes, peeled, cubed

1 can (14½ ounces [406 g]) diced tomatoes (I use Muir Glen diced tomatoes), undrained

2 cups (474 mL) chicken broth (Pacific Natural Foods chicken broth is gluten free)

½ cup (119 mL) orange juice

1 tablespoon grated orange zest

½ teaspoon ground ginger

½ cup sour cream (beware low-fat varieties, as they may contain food starches—check labels carefully)

Salt and pepper, to taste

4 cups (760 g) cooked brown basmati rice, warm

1. Sauté the chicken, onions, bell peppers, and garlic in oil in a large saucepan until the chicken is browned and the vegetables are tender, for 8 to 10 minutes. Add the squash, potatoes, tomatoes with liquid, broth, orange juice and zest, and ginger; heat to boiling. Reduce the heat and simmer, uncovered, for 30 minutes. Reduce the heat to low and stir in the sour cream; season to taste with the salt and pepper. Serve immediately over the rice.

SAUCES

TRADITIONAL WHITE ROUX

Roux is a kitchen classic. It's the foundation of a wide variety of sauces, soups, main dishes, hors d'oeuvres, and desserts, and you won't want to be without it in your repertoire. It's traditionally made with wheat flour, but sweet rice flour is an acceptable substitute.

WHITE ROUX

2 tablespoons butter or butter substitute
2 tablespoons sweet rice flour
1 cup (237 mL) milk or broth (Pacific Natural Foods chicken broth is gluten free)

1. Melt the butter in a medium-sized, heavy saucepan over low heat. Sprinkle in the flour and stir until completely together. Cook slowly, stirring constantly for 2 minutes, and until pasty and solid.

2. Gradually stir in the milk or broth. Increase the heat to medium and cook, whisking constantly, until the sauce is smooth and thick and reaches the boiling point. Reduce the heat. Add salt and pepper, to taste. Use as needed.

VARIATION

Traditional Brown Roux—Use the same ingredients listed in the White Roux recipe above. Melt the butter in a medium-sized, heavy saucepan over low heat. Sprinkle in the sweet rice flour and stir until completely blended. Cook slowly, stirring constantly for 3 to 5 minutes, until the mixture has a pasty consistency and is nutty brown in color. Gradually stir in the milk or broth. Increase the heat to medium and cook, whisking constantly, until the sauce is smooth and thick and reaches the boiling point. Reduce the heat. Add salt and pepper, to taste. Use as needed in gravy, Creole gumbos, stews, and other sauces.

DAIRY-FREE AND VEGAN ROUX

2 tablespoons olive oil or butter substitute
1 tablespoon potato starch
1 cup (237 mL) soy milk or broth

1. Completely melt the oil in a medium-sized, heavy saucepan over low heat. Mix the potato starch into the oil, stirring constantly. Cook for 1 minute (unlike a traditional roux that is pasty, this roux will be foamy).

2. Gradually stir in the broth. Increase the heat to medium and cook, whisking constantly, until the sauce is smooth and thick and reaches the boiling point. Reduce the heat. Add salt and pepper, to taste. Use as needed.

BARBECUE SAUCE

This recipe is adapted from The Gluten-Free Good Health Cookbook *by Annalise G. Roberts and Dr. Claudia Pillow.*

1 (8-ounce [227-g]) can fire roasted tomatoes, puréed (I prefer Muir Glen)
1 cup (150 g) chopped onions
2 tablespoons molasses
1 tablespoon minced garlic
1 teaspoon dried oregano
2 teaspoons ground cumin
2 teaspoons chili powder (I prefer McCormick's spices, because they always list flour on the ingredient label if it's included—check the label carefully to ensure your chili powder is gluten free)
Salt and freshly ground black pepper

1. Combine the tomatoes, chopped onions, molasses, garlic, oregano, cumin, chili powder in a small bowl. Add the salt and pepper, to taste. It can be chilled in the refrigerator.

CITRUS BEURRE BLANC

This recipe is adapted from The Gluten-Free Good Health Cookbook *by Annalise G. Roberts and Dr. Claudia Pillow.*

> 1 tablespoon granulated sugar
> 1½ teaspoons white wine vinegar
> 1 cup (237 mL) orange juice
> ¼ cup (38 g) minced shallots
> ½ teaspoon minced garlic
> ½ cup (119 mL) dry white wine
> ½ cup (119 mL) chicken broth (Pacific Natural Foods
>   chicken broth is gluten free)
> Juice of 1 lime
> 1 tablespoon unsalted butter
> 1 tablespoon chopped fresh cilantro
> Dash Tabasco sauce
> Salt and freshly ground black pepper

1. Put the sugar and vinegar in a small saucepan and whisk to combine. Cook over medium-high heat until the sugar/vinegar mixture becomes a light caramel color.

2. Whisk in the orange juice and bring to a boil. Reduce the heat to medium and allow the mixture to reduce by half (about ½ cup [119 mL]), whisking occasionally. Set aside.

3. Combine the shallots, garlic, white wine, broth, and lime juice in a small sauté pan. Bring to a boil over medium-high heat until the mixture is reduced to ¼ cup (59 mL) of liquid. Whisk in the orange juice mixture and the butter. Stir in the cilantro and Tabasco sauce. Season with the salt and pepper, to taste.

MAPLE MUSTARD SAUCE

This recipe is adapted from The Gluten-Free Good Health Cookbook *by Annalise G. Roberts and Dr. Claudia Pillow.*

> 1 teaspoon dried sage or 1 tablespoon fresh chopped sage
> 1 cup (237 mL) chicken broth (Pacific Natural Foods chicken broth is gluten free)
> 4 teaspoons pure maple syrup
> 4 teaspoons coarse-grain mustard
> Salt and freshly ground black pepper

1. Whisk together the broth, maple syrup, mustard, and sage. Pour into a saucepan and boil until syrupy, for about 2 minutes. Remove from the heat. Season to taste with more salt and pepper.

CUCUMBER RAITA

This recipe is adapted from The Gluten-Free Good Health Cookbook *by Annalise G. Roberts and Dr. Claudia Pillow.*

> 1 cup (237 mL) plain Greek yogurt (Chobani is gluten free)
> ¼ cup (42 g) cucumber, peeled, seeded, and cut into small cubes
> 1 tablespoon chopped fresh cilantro
> 1 teaspoon chopped fresh mint leaves
> ½ teaspoon ground cumin
> ½ teaspoon salt
> Freshly ground black pepper
> ⅛ teaspoon cayenne pepper

1. Pour the yogurt into a small mixing bowl and beat with a fork until smooth. Add the cucumber, cilantro, mint, cumin, salt, black pepper, and cayenne pepper. Mix well and chill before using.

FRESH TOMATO AND HERB SAUCE >

5 cups (800 g) chopped tomatoes

½ cup (75 g) chopped onion

½ cup (119 mL) dry red wine or water

2 tablespoons tomato paste

2 tablespoons minced garlic

2 tablespoons finely chopped fresh or 1½ teaspoons dried thyme leaves

1 tablespoon sugar

2 bay leaves

⅛ teaspoon crushed red pepper

⅛ teaspoon ground black pepper

½ teaspoon salt

3–4 tablespoons (5–6 g) finely chopped fresh or 2 teaspoons dried basil leaves

1. Combine all the ingredients, except the basil, in a large saucepan; heat to boiling. Reduce the heat and simmer, covered, for 5 minutes. Simmer, uncovered, until the sauce is reduced to a medium consistency, for about 30 minutes, adding the basil during last 5 minutes. Discard the bay leaves.

SOUR CREAM AND POBLANO SAUCE

This recipe comes from 1,001 Best Low-Fat Recipes *by Sue Spitler.*

   1 thinly sliced large poblano chili
   1 finely chopped small onion
   2 cloves garlic, minced
   1 cup (237 mL) sour cream (beware low-fat varieties, as
      they may contain food starches—check labels carefully)
   ¼ teaspoon ground cumin
   Salt and pepper, to taste

1. Sauté the poblano chili, onion, and garlic in a lightly greased small saucepan until very tender, for about 5 minutes. Stir in the sour cream and cumin; cook over low heat 2 to 3 minutes. Season to taste with the salt and pepper.

BÉARNAISE SAUCE

   6 ounces (170 g) cream cheese
   ⅓ cup (79 mL) sour cream (beware low-fat varieties, as
      they may contain food starches—check labels carefully)
   3–4 tablespoons (45–60 mL) 2% milk
   2 teaspoons minced shallot
   2 teaspoons lemon juice
   ½–1 teaspoon Dijon mustard
   1½ teaspoons dried tarragon leaves
   Salt and white pepper, to taste

1. Combine all the ingredients except the salt and pepper. Transfer the mixture to a small saucepan over medium-low heat and heat until melted and smooth, stirring constantly. Season to taste with the salt and pepper.

RED BEAN SAUCE

This recipe is adapted from The Gluten-Free Good Health Cookbook *by Annalise G. Roberts and Dr. Claudia Pillow.*

> 2 teaspoons canola oil
> 1 dried ancho chili pepper
> ½ cup (75 g) chopped onions
> ½ cup (64 g) finely chopped carrots
> 2 teaspoons minced garlic
> 1 (15.5-ounce [434-g]) can red kidney beans, drained and rinsed
> 1 cup (237 mL) chicken broth (Pacific Natural Foods chicken broth is gluten free)
> 2 teaspoons ground cumin
> 1 tablespoon freshly chopped cilantro
> ½ teaspoon salt
> ½ teaspoon coarsely ground black pepper

1. Heat the oil in a medium-sized, heavy saucepan over medium heat. Add the dried ancho chili pepper and cook for 1 minute, until softened. Add the onions, carrots, and garlic and cook until the onions are tender, for about 5 minutes. Add the beans, chicken broth, cumin, salt, and pepper. Cover and simmer for 20 minutes. Remove and discard the ancho chili pepper.

2. Remove the bean mixture from the heat and purée in a blender. Reheat in a small saucepan or microwave as necessary; add the cilantro and more salt, and pepper, to taste.

CHILI TOMATO SAUCE

1 cup (237 mL) tomato sauce (Hunt's is gluten free)

2 tablespoons water

1–1½ tablespoons chili powder (I prefer McCormick's spices, because they always list flour on the ingredient label if it's included—check the label carefully to ensure your chili powder is gluten free)

1 clove garlic

Salt and pepper, to taste

1. Heat all the ingredients, except the salt and pepper, to boiling in a small saucepan. Reduce the heat and simmer, uncovered, for 2 to 3 minutes. Season to taste with the salt and pepper.

PASILLA CHILI SAUCE

3 pasilla chilies
2 medium tomatoes, coarsely chopped
1 small onion, coarsely chopped
½ teaspoon sugar
1 cup (237 mL) sour cream (beware low-fat varieties, as
   they may contain food starches—check labels carefully)
Salt and pepper, to taste

1. Cook the chilies in a lightly greased small skillet over medium heat until soft; remove and discard the stems, seeds, and veins. Process the chilies, tomatoes, onion, and sugar in a blender until smooth. Cook the mixture in a lightly greased medium skillet over medium heat until thickened, for about 5 minutes. Reduce the heat to low; stir in the sour cream and cook until hot, for about 2 minutes. Season to taste with the salt and pepper.

TOMATILLO SAUCE

1½ pounds (681 g) tomatillos, husked
½ cup (75 g) chopped onion
1 teaspoon chopped garlic
1 teaspoon serrano chili
3 tablespoons (3 g) chopped cilantro
2–3 teaspoons sugar
Salt and white pepper, to taste

1. Cook the tomatillos in 2 inches (5 cm) of simmering water in a large saucepan until tender, for 5 to 8 minutes; drain and cool.

2. Process the tomatillos, onion, garlic, chili, and cilantro in a food processor or blender until almost smooth. Heat the sauce to boiling in a lightly greased large skillet.

3. Reduce the heat and simmer until slightly thickened, for about 5 minutes. Season to taste with the sugar, salt, and pepper.

VERACRUZ SAUCE

1 cup (150 g) chopped onion

3 cloves garlic, minced

1 pickled jalapeño chili, minced

2-inch (5-cm) piece cinnamon stick

1 bay leaf

½ teaspoon dried oregano leaves

½ teaspoon dried thyme leaves

½ teaspoon ground cumin

3 cups (480 g) chopped tomatoes

¼ cup (34 g) sliced pitted green olives

1–2 tablespoons capers

Salt and pepper, to taste

1. Sauté the onion, garlic, jalapeño chili, cinnamon, and herbs in a large lightly greased skillet until onion is tender, for 5 to 8 minutes. Add the tomatoes, olives, and capers; simmer, uncovered, until the sauce is of a medium consistency, for about 10 minutes. Discard the bay leaf; season to taste with the salt and pepper.

CHICKEN

THAI CHICKEN

This dish is comforting and fast—ready in less than 20 minutes. Spice up the week and savor the flavor. This recipe is adapted from The Gluten-Free Good Health Cookbook *by Annalise G. Roberts and Dr. Claudia Pillow.*

3–4 SERVINGS

2 tablespoons organic coconut oil

1 pound (454 g) boneless, skinless chicken breasts, cut into 2-inch (5-cm) thin strips

1 (14-ounce [420-mL]) can coconut milk

½ cup (60 g) diced celery

2 tablespoons red curry paste (Thai Kitchen's is gluten free)

3 tablespoons (45 mL) fish sauce (Thai Kitchen's is gluten free)

1 tablespoon brown sugar

1 tablespoon chopped fresh basil

½ cup (75 g) scallions, finely chopped

¼ cup (4 g) chopped fresh cilantro

Cooked brown basmati rice, for serving

1. Heat the oil in a large, heavy saucepan over medium-high heat. Sauté the chicken strips until lightly browned, for about 3 to 5 minutes. Stir in the coconut milk, celery, and red curry paste; simmer for 5 minutes.

2. Reduce the heat to medium-low and stir in the fish sauce, brown sugar, and basil. Cook for 5 minutes.

3. Remove from the heat. Sprinkle with the scallions and cilantro and serve immediately over the rice.

GRILLED CHICKEN WITH LEMON, ROSEMARY, AND GARLIC

This recipe requires very little in the way of preparation, but the result is tender, flavorful chicken every time. It makes a delicious outdoor meal when served with grilled vegetables or a colorful bean salad. This recipe is adapted from The Gluten-Free Good Health Cookbook *by Annalise G. Roberts and Dr. Claudia Pillow.*

6 SERVINGS

⅓ cup (79 mL) olive oil

2 tablespoons balsamic vinegar

1 teaspoon dried thyme

½ teaspoon sea salt

¼ cup (59 mL) fresh lemon juice

3 tablespoons (6 g) chopped fresh rosemary

1 tablespoon grated fresh lemon zest

2 teaspoons minced garlic

½ teaspoon freshly ground black pepper

2 pounds (908 g) boneless, skinless chicken breasts, cut in half

1. Combine the oil, vinegar, thyme, salt, lemon juice, rosemary, lemon zest, garlic, and pepper in a large bowl and mix well.

2. Place the chicken in a bowl and pour in the marinade. Toss to coat with the marinade. Let the chicken marinate at room temperature for 30 minutes or cover and refrigerate for at least 1 hour (overnight is best), turning occasionally.

3. Preheat and prepare the grill. Grill the chicken over medium heat, basting occasionally with the marinade. Cook for 15 to 20 minutes, or until done, turning every 5 minutes. Transfer to a clean serving platter and serve immediately.

CORN MEAL-CRUSTED CHICKEN >

These crisp, crunchy cutlets can be ready in less than 20 minutes and are delicious with ready-made salsa or chutney. Serve them alongside whatever vegetables you have on hand for a colorful, healthy dinner everyone will enjoy. This recipe is adapted from The Gluten-Free Good Health Cookbook *by Annalise G. Roberts and Dr. Claudia Pillow.*

4 SERVINGS

> 4 boneless, skinless chicken breasts (about 1½ pounds [681 g])
> ¼ cup (40 g) brown rice flour (Bob's Red Mill is a good choice)
> 1 large egg, beaten
> ⅔ cup (106 g) corn meal
> 1 teaspoon chili powder
> Salt and freshly ground black pepper
> 2 tablespoons organic coconut oil or canola oil
> Ready-made gluten-free salsa or chutney (Stonewall Kitchens' Major Grey's chutney is gluten free), for serving

1. Place each chicken breast between 2 pieces of wax paper (or plastic wrap) and pound to ½-inch (13-mm) thickness with a meat mallet or rolling pin.

2. Place the brown rice flour, egg, and corn meal each in separate shallow dishes. Mix the chili powder with the corn meal.

3. Sprinkle each breast with salt and pepper and dredge each lightly in the brown rice flour. Dip each breast in the beaten egg, coating it completely. Dip and coat each breast in the corn meal. Place the breasts on a platter.

4. Heat the oil in a large, heavy skillet over medium heat. Place the chicken in the skillet and cook for about 2 to 3 minutes on each side, until the coating is crisp and the chicken is cooked through. Serve immediately with the salsa or chutney.

CHICKEN PARMESAN

Here is a tried-and-true version of a true classic. You can make it ahead and gently rewarm it covered with foil in a preheated 350°F (180°C) oven. Enjoy your meal with gluten-free pasta and a large green salad. This recipe is adapted from The Gluten-Free Good Health Cookbook *by Annalise G. Roberts and Dr. Claudia Pillow.*

4 SERVINGS

4 boneless, skinless chicken breasts (about 1½ pounds [681 g])

¼ cup (40 g) brown rice flour (Bob's Red Mill is a good choice)

⅛ teaspoon black pepper

⅛ teaspoon salt

1 large egg, lightly beaten

¾ cup (113 g) gluten-free bread crumbs (I recommend Glutino and Schar brands)

½ teaspoon oregano

½ teaspoon basil

¼ cup (25 g) grated Parmesan cheese (grate your own to ensure no wheat products are added to prevent caking)

1 tablespoon extra virgin olive oil

1½ cups (356 mL) favorite prepared tomato sauce

1 cup (114 g) shredded mozzarella cheese (shred your own to ensure no wheat products are added to prevent caking)

1 cup (114 g) shredded provolone cheese (shred your own to ensure no wheat products are added to prevent caking)

2 tablespoons chopped fresh parsley, for sprinkling

2 tablespoons chopped fresh basil, for sprinkling

1. Preheat the oven to 400°F (200°C). Place the rack in the center of the oven. Grease an 11- × 7-inch (27.5- x 17.5-cm) baking dish with cooking spray or brush with olive oil.

2. Place each chicken breast between 2 sheets of wax paper (or plastic wrap) and pound to ½-inch (13-mm) thickness with a meat mallet or rolling pin.

3. Combine the brown rice flour, pepper, and salt in a flat dish. Place the beaten egg in a shallow dish. Combine the bread crumbs, oregano, basil, and Parmesan cheese in a shallow dish.

4. Dredge the chicken breasts in the brown rice flour and then dip them in the beaten egg. Next, dredge the breasts in the bread crumb mixture. Place the breasts on a platter.

5. Heat the oil in a large, heavy skillet over medium-high heat. Add the chicken and sauté for 1 to 2 minutes on each side or until golden brown. Remove from the heat.

6. Spread ½ cup (119 mL) of the tomato sauce in the prepared baking dish. Arrange the chicken breasts in a single layer on top of the sauce. Top each piece with ¼ cup (59 mL) of the sauce. Sprinkle with the mozzarella and provolone cheese.

7. Bake for 10 minutes, or until the cheese is melted and bubbling slightly. Sprinkle with the parsley and basil and serve immediately.

CHICKEN BREAST ROLL-UPS WITH PROSCIUTTO AND PECORINO CHEESE

The prosciutto gives this simple dish richness and makes it perfect even for fancy dinners. Speck is similar to prosciutto but usually a little more moist. Use speck if possible, as it tends to dry out less and has the same rich flavor as prosciutto. This recipe comes from The Puglian Cookbook *by Viktorija Todorovska.*

4 SERVINGS

> 4 chicken breast filets, pounded to ¼ inch (6 mm) thickness
>
> 4 slices prosciutto or speck (Boar's Head meats are all gluten free)
>
> 1 cup (100 g) grated pecorino cheese (a sheep's milk cheese similar to Parmigiano-Reggiano; grate your own to ensure no wheat products are added to prevent caking)
>
> 3 tablespoons (45 mL) extra virgin olive oil
>
> 1 cup (236 mL) dry white wine
>
> Salt, to taste

1. On a clean working surface, spread out the pounded chicken filets. Cover each with a slice of prosciutto and sprinkle with ¼ of the pecorino cheese. Roll up each filet and close it with a toothpick. Set aside.

2. In a large pan, heat the olive oil over medium-high heat. Add the roll-ups and cook for about 3 minutes on each side, until they are well browned on all sides. Add the wine, scrape the bottom of the pan to loosen any pieces of meat, reduce the heat, and cook for 10 minutes. Add salt, to taste. Serve immediately.

CHICKEN BREASTS WITH BALSAMIC VINEGAR AND ROSEMARY

Easy, yet elegant, this delicious entrée is good served with brown rice and a simple vegetable or salad.

4 SERVINGS

> 1 tablespoon olive oil
>
> 1½ teaspoons balsamic vinegar
>
> 1 teaspoon minced garlic
>
> 1 tablespoon finely grated lemon zest
>
> ¼ teaspoon salt
>
> ¼ teaspoon pepper
>
> 4 boneless, skinless chicken breast halves (4 ounces [114 g] each)
>
> ½–¾ cup (119–178 mL) dry white wine or chicken broth (Pacific Natural Foods chicken broth is gluten free)
>
> ½ cup (80 g) chopped tomato
>
> 1 teaspoon finely chopped fresh or ½ teaspoon dried rosemary leaves

1. Combine the olive oil, vinegar, garlic, lemon zest, salt, and pepper and brush the mixture over the chicken; let stand 10 minutes. Cook the chicken in a lightly greased large skillet over medium heat until browned, for about 5 minutes on each side.

2. Add the wine, tomato, and rosemary to the skillet and heat to boiling. Reduce the heat and simmer, covered, until the chicken is cooked, for about 15 minutes. Serve immediately.

SPAGHETTI SQUASH STUFFED WITH CHICKEN AND VEGETABLES

Jerusalem artichokes, or sun chokes, add extra crunch to the sautéed vegetables.

4 SERVINGS

2 medium spaghetti squash (about 2 pounds [908 g] each), halved lengthwise, seeded

12 ounces (341 g) boneless, skinless chicken breast, cubed

8 ounces (227 g) Jerusalem artichokes, cubed, peeled

1½ cups (113 g) quartered mushrooms

½ cup (60 g) sliced celery

½ cup (64 g) sliced carrot

½ cup (75 g) chopped onion

2 cloves garlic, minced

2 teaspoons brown rice flour (Bob's Red Mill is a good choice)

2 medium tomatoes, coarsely chopped

½ cup (119 mL) chicken broth (Pacific Natural Foods chicken broth is gluten free)

1 teaspoon dried marjoram leaves

Salt and pepper, to taste

2 green onions, thinly sliced

1. Place the squash halves, cut sides down, in a large baking pan; add ½ inch (13 mm) of water. Bake, covered, at 350°F (180°C) until the squash is tender, for 30 to 40 minutes. Scrape the pulp into a large bowl, separating the strands with a fork; reserve the shells.

2. Sauté the chicken, Jerusalem artichokes, mushrooms, celery, carrot, onion, and garlic in a lightly greased large skillet until the chicken is light brown, for about 8 minutes. Stir in the brown rice flour and cook for 1 minute.

3. Add the tomatoes, broth, and marjoram; heat to boiling. Cook, covered, until the vegetables are tender, for about 10 minutes. Season to taste with the salt and pepper. Toss the mixture with the squash; spoon into the reserved squash shells. Sprinkle with the green onions. Serve immediately.

CHICKEN AND CHEESE RELLENOS >

This healthy version of chili rellenos eliminates the customary egg coating and frying in oil. This recipe comes from 1,001 Best Low-Fat Recipes *by Sue Spitler.*

6 SERVINGS

> 6 large poblano chilies
> 1 chopped medium onion
> 1 chopped carrot
> 1 chopped garlic clove
> 1 pound (454 g) boneless, skinless chicken breast, cooked, shredded
> ½ cup (80 g) whole kernel corn
> ½ teaspoon ground cumin
> ½ teaspoon dried thyme leaves
> ½ cup (57 g) shredded Monterey Jack cheese (shred your own to ensure no wheat products are added)
> ½ cup (57 g) shredded Cheddar cheese (shred your own to ensure no wheat products are added to prevent caking)
> Salt and pepper, to taste
> 1 tablespoon vegetable oil
> Chili Tomato Sauce (see recipe page 64)

1. Cut the stems from the tops of the chilies; remove and discard the seeds and veins. Simmer the peppers, covered in water, until slightly softened, for 2 to 3 minutes; drain and cool.

2. Sauté the onion, carrot, and garlic in a lightly greased large skillet until tender, for 3 to 5 minutes. Add the chicken, corn, and herbs; cook over medium heat for 1 to 2 minutes. Remove from the heat and stir in the cheeses; season to taste with the salt and pepper. Spoon the mixture into the peppers; sauté in the oil in a large skillet until tender and browned on all sides, for 6 to 8 minutes. Serve immediately with the Chili Tomato Sauce.

CHICKEN AND VEGETABLE CURRY

A variety of spices and herbs combine to make the fragrant curry that seasons this dish.

4 SERVINGS

12–16 ounces (341–454 g) boneless, skinless chicken breast, cubed

½ cup (75 g) chopped onion

2 cloves garlic

1 tablespoon brown rice flour (Bob's Red Mill is a good choice)

1 small head cauliflower, cut into florets

1 cup (150 g) cubed, peeled fresh potatoes

1 cup (160 g) chopped tomato

1 cup (128 g) thickly sliced carrots

1½ cups (356 mL) chicken broth (Pacific Natural Foods chicken broth is gluten free)

¾ teaspoon ground turmeric

¼ teaspoon dry mustard

¼ teaspoon ground cumin

¼ teaspoon ground coriander

1–2 tablespoons lemon juice

Salt and cayenne pepper, to taste

1. Sauté the chicken, onion, and garlic in a lightly greased large saucepan until the chicken is browned, for 5 to 6 minutes; stir in the brown rice flour and cook for 1 minute.

2. Add the vegetables, broth, and herbs; heat to boiling. Reduce the heat and simmer, covered, until the chicken and vegetables are tender, for 10 to 15 minutes. Season to taste with the lemon juice, salt, and cayenne pepper. Serve immediately.

MEATS

BEEF STROGANOFF

Beef Stroganoff is a dramatic, dairy-free dish that you can count on to make the people around your table happy. This recipe is adapted from The Gluten-Free Good Health Cookbook *by Annalise G. Roberts and Dr. Claudia Pillow.*

8–10 SERVINGS

2 tablespoons organic coconut oil or olive oil, divided

½ cup (75 g) minced onion

½ pound (227 g) mushrooms, sliced

1 teaspoon thyme

Salt and freshly ground pepper

3 pounds (1.36 kg) beef tenderloin, trimmed and cut into 1-inch by 2-inch (2.5-cm by 5-cm) pieces

1 cup (237 mL) beef broth or stock (Swanson's Beef Stock is gluten free)

1 rounded teaspoon beef demi-glace (Savory Choice makes great gluten-free demi-glace)

1 tablespoon potato starch

1 cup (237 mL) canned coconut milk

Cooked buttered gluten-free pasta, for serving (Tinkyada makes good gluten-free pasta)

1. Heat 1 tablespoon of the oil over medium heat in a large, heavy skillet. Sauté the onions until golden brown and tender. Add the mushrooms and thyme and continue cooking until the mushrooms are tender and have released their juices. Set aside in a bowl. Season with the salt and pepper, to taste.

2. Season the beef with salt and pepper. Heat ½ tablespoon of the oil over high heat in the same skillet. Brown half of the beef (about 3 minutes). The beef should be rosy inside; set aside in another bowl. Add the remaining oil to the skillet and repeat with the other half of the beef. Set aside in bowl.

3. Reduce the heat to medium. Deglaze the pan with the beef broth. Add the demi-glace. Stir to combine the demi-glace and cook until the liquid is reduced to ⅔ cup (158 mL), for about 3 to 4 minutes. Stir the potato starch into the coconut milk and add to the skillet. Stir to combine into the sauce; simmer 2 minutes. Do not boil.

4. Add the mushrooms and any accumulated sauce back to the skillet; simmer for 1 minute. Add the beef and any accumulated sauce back to the skillet and stir to coat the beef with the sauce; simmer for 1 minute to rewarm. Add more salt and pepper, to taste. Serve immediately with the pasta.

SOUTHWESTERN BRAISED CHUCK ROAST >

Start this dish early in the afternoon so the whole house fills with delectable aromas. Serve it with mashed potatoes and plenty of fresh, steamed vegetables to soak up the thick sauce. This recipe is adapted from The Gluten-Free Good Health Cookbook *by Annalise G. Roberts and Dr. Claudia Pillow.*

8 SERVINGS

2 tablespoons olive oil

5 (2.27 kg) pounds chuck roast

Salt and freshly ground black pepper

1 tablespoon minced garlic

1 cup (150 g) chopped onion

1 cup (120 g) chopped celery

1 cup (150 g) chopped red bell pepper

1 cup (128 g) sliced carrot, cut into 2-inch (5-cm) pieces

1 small jalapeño pepper, seeded, finely chopped

½ cup (119 mL) red wine or beef broth

1 tablespoon molasses

1 ancho chili, whole

2 teaspoons dried oregano

1 teaspoon ground cumin

1 cup strong freshly brewed coffee (not espresso or dark roast; be sure the coffee is gluten free)

1 (14.5-ounce [406 g]) can diced tomatoes (I use Muir Glen diced tomatoes), undrained

1 tablespoon tomato paste

¼ cup (4 g) chopped fresh cilantro, for sprinkling

1. Heat the oil in a large, heavy saucepan over medium-high heat. Sprinkle the chuck roast with the salt and pepper and add to the saucepan. Brown for 4 minutes per side. Transfer to a platter.

2. Add the garlic, onion, celery, red bell pepper, carrot, and jalapeño pepper to the saucepan. Reduce the heat to medium, cover, and cook until the onion is tender, stirring occasionally, for about 5 minutes. Add the red wine and stir for 15 seconds. Add the molasses, ancho chile, oregano, cumin, coffee, tomatoes with juice, and tomato paste. Bring to a boil while scraping up the browned bits. Return the chuck and any juices to the pan and bring to a boil.

3. Cover, reduce the heat to low, and simmer until the meat is very tender, for about 2 hours. Turn the chuck every 30 minutes while simmering. Season with more salt and pepper. Transfer the chuck to a platter.

4. Purée the sauce in a food processor (or with a hand processor) and then pour the sauce over the chuck. Sprinkle with the chopped cilantro and serve immediately.

Note: Can be prepared 1 day ahead. Cool and cover with foil. Refrigerate until needed. Rewarm, covered in the oven, for 30 to 40 minutes at 350°F (180°C).

BRISKET WITH BARBECUE SAUCE

Try this brisket with its own savory barbecue sauce for a weekend dinner with family or friends. Enjoy the leftovers on Monday for another quick and easy meal. This recipe is adapted from The Gluten-Free Good Health Cookbook *by Annalise G. Roberts and Dr. Claudia Pillow.*

6–8 SERVINGS

1 tablespoon olive oil
1 4-pound (1.82-kg) flat-cut beef brisket, trimmed
Barbecue Sauce (see recipe page 57)
Salt and freshly ground black pepper

1. Place the rack in the center of the oven. Preheat the oven to 325°F (160°C).

2. Heat the oil in a large, heavy (5-quart [4.74-L]) Dutch oven or other large, covered, ovenproof pot over very high heat; brown the meat on both sides.

3. Pour the Barbecue Sauce over the meat. Add the salt and pepper, to taste.

4. Cover the pot and place it in the oven. Cook for about 3 hours or until fork tender, turning once every hour.

5. Transfer the brisket to a plate or cutting board and allow it to cool for 1 hour. Trim any remaining fat and thinly slice across the grain. Return the meat to the pot and arrange the slices in the sauce in order to reheat. Rewarm, covered, in a preheated 350°F (180°C) oven and serve with the pan sauce.

MUSTARD ROAST BEEF

The spicy coating makes this roast beef extra juicy and flavorful.

¼ cup (80 g) apricot preserves (Smuckers is gluten free)

2–4 tablespoons (30–60 mL) spicy brown mustard (French's is gluten free)

2–3 teaspoons Worcestershire sauce (Lea & Perrins is gluten free)

1 tablespoon light brown sugar

1 tablespoon prepared horseradish (Bubbies brand is gluten free)

1 teaspoon crushed caraway seeds

1 teaspoon black peppercorns

¼ teaspoon ground allspice (I prefer McCormick's spices, because they always list flour on the ingredient label if it's included—check the label carefully to ensure your allspice is gluten free)

1 boneless beef sirloin tip roast, fat trimmed (about 2 pounds [908 g])

1. Mix all the ingredients, except the beef; spread on all the surfaces of the beef. Place the beef on a rack in a roasting pan; roast at 325°F (160°C) to desired doneness, 160°F (71°C) for medium, for 45 to 60 minutes. Let stand for 10 minutes before slicing. Serve hot.

MEXICAN HASH

Leftover meat or poultry can be used in this dish. Serve with fried eggs for a heartier meal.

4 SERVINGS

1 pound (454 g) beef eye of round, fat trimmed, cubed
1 cup (160 g) chopped tomato
1 cup (150 g) onion
2 large poblano chilies, sliced
1 pound (454 g) Idaho potatoes, unpeeled, cooked, cubed
Chili powder, to taste (I prefer McCormick's spices, because they always list flour on the ingredient label if it's included—check the label carefully to ensure your chili powder is gluten free)
Salt and pepper, to taste

1. Cook the beef in 2 inches of simmering water in a large saucepan, covered, until the beef is tender, for 20 to 25 minutes; drain. Cool slightly and shred. Sauté the beef in a lightly greased large skillet over until it is beginning to brown and crisp, for about 5 minutes. Add the tomato; cook over medium heat for 5 minutes. Remove from the skillet.

2. Add the onion and poblano chilies to the skillet; cook until tender, for 5 to 8 minutes. Add the potatoes and cook until browned, for about 5 minutes. Add the reserved meat mixture to the skillet and cook until hot, for 3 to 4 minutes. Season to taste with the chili powder, salt, and pepper. Serve immediately.

SLOW-BRAISED PULLED PORK

Melt-in-your-mouth tender and delicately spiced, this Slow-Braised Pulled Pork is one of those dishes our families eagerly anticipate. It should be started early on the day you plan to serve it—or better yet, the day before. This recipe is adapted from The Gluten-Free Good Health Cookbook *by Annalise G. Roberts and Dr. Claudia Pillow.*

8 SERVINGS

1 tablespoon olive oil

1 (5½-pound [2.5-kg]) pork shoulder rump roast

½ cup (119 mL) beef broth or stock (Swanson's Beef Stock is gluten free)

1 tablespoon tomato paste

1 tablespoon minced fresh garlic

1 teaspoon ground cumin

1 teaspoon chili powder (I prefer McCormick's spices, because they always list flour on the ingredient label if it's included—check the label carefully to ensure your chili powder is gluten free)

1 teaspoon dried thyme

1 teaspoon sea salt

1 teaspoon freshly ground black pepper

¼ cup chopped fresh cilantro, for sprinkling

Red Bean Sauce (see recipe on page 63), for serving

1. Place the rack in the center of the oven. Preheat the oven to 325°F (160°C).

2. Heat the oil in a large, heavy (5-quart [4.74-L]) Dutch oven or other large, covered, ovenproof pot over very high heat; brown the meat on all sides.

3. Pour in the broth and add the tomato paste, garlic, cumin, chili powder, thyme, salt, and pepper.

4.	Cover the pot and place it in the oven. Baste and turn the meat every 45 minutes. Cook for 3 to 4 hours, or until the meat is fork tender and falling apart and the gravy is reduced. If the pot has a tight seal and the gravy isn't reducing, remove the lid for the last 1½ hours of cooking time.

5.	Allow the meat to cool in the pot uncovered. Remove the meat and cut into chunks. Return the meat to the pot in order to reheat, or store in a tightly sealed container in the refrigerator. Rewarm, covered, in the oven for 30 to 40 minutes, or until hot, at 350°F (180°C). Serve immediately sprinkled with the fresh cilantro and Red Bean Sauce or with a favorite barbecue sauce (Stubb's is great and gluten free).

SAUTÉED PORK WITH MAPLE MUSTARD SAUCE

Pork with Maple Mustard Sauce pairs sweet maple syrup with spicy country mustard for a delectable pork dish you and your family will relish. This recipe is adapted from The Gluten-Free Good Health Cookbook *by Annalise G. Roberts and Dr. Claudia Pillow.*

4–6 SERVINGS

> 1½ pounds (681 g) pork tenderloin (or pork cutlets—if using cutlets, skip Steps 1 and 2)
> Salt and freshly ground black pepper
> ½ teaspoon dried thyme, divided
> ½ teaspoon dried sage, divided
> 2 tablespoons olive oil, divided
> Maple Mustard Sauce (see recipe page 59)

1. Trim the tenderloins and cut them into 1-inch-thick (2.5-cm-thick) slices.

2. Place each pork slice between sheets of wax paper (or plastic wrap) and pound them to a ¼-inch (6-mm) thickness with a mallet or rolling pin.

3. Lay the pork slices on a plate and sprinkle with salt, pepper, and ¼ teaspoon each of the thyme and sage. Turn them over and repeat, sprinkling with salt, pepper, and the remaining ¼ teaspoon each of the thyme and sage. Set aside. Cover tightly with plastic wrap and refrigerate. (It can be prepared up to 3 hours ahead.)

4. Melt 1 tablespoon of the oil in a large skillet over medium-high heat. Add half the pork slices and sauté for about 2 minutes per side, until browned and cooked through. Transfer to a plate and cover loosely with foil. Repeat with the remaining oil and pork slices. Transfer the cooked pork slices to the foil-covered plate.

5. Pour the Maple Mustard Sauce on the slices. Serve immediately.

PORK MEDALLIONS WITH APPLES AND YOGURT SAUCE

Pork baked with apples and yogurt makes a light and amazingly easy dinner. This recipe comes from 1,001 Best Low-Fat Recipes by Sue Spitler.

4 SERVINGS

- 1 pound (454 g) pork tenderloin, sliced (½-inch [13-mm])
- 2 cups (380 g) cooked brown or white long-grain rice
- 2 medium Granny Smith apples, sliced (½-inch [13-mm])
- ½ cup (119 mL) apple juice
- 1 small onion, finely chopped
- ¼ teaspoon salt
- ½ teaspoon dried sage leaves
- 2 tablespoons brown rice flour (Bob's Red Mill is a good choice)
- 1 cup (237 mL) plain Greek yogurt (Chobani is gluten free)
- 1 tablespoon chopped chives or parsley

1. Arrange the pork slices over the rice in a greased baking dish, overlapping the slices if necessary; arrange the apples on top. Heat the apple juice, onion, salt, and sage to boiling in a small skillet. Reduce the heat and simmer, covered, until the onion is tender, for about 5 minutes. Whisk in the combined brown rice flour and yogurt, whisking until thickened, for about 1 minute. Spoon the sauce over the pork and apples; sprinkle with the chives and bake at 325°F (160°C), covered, until the pork is slightly pink, for 45 to 60 minutes. Serve immediately.

CHORIZO

Serve Chorizo as patties, or cook and crumble to serve in quesadillas, enchiladas, and other dishes.

4 SERVINGS

¼ teaspoon crushed coriander and cumin seeds

1 dried ancho chili

12 ounces (341 g) pork tenderloin, finely chopped or ground

1 tablespoon paprika

1 tablespoon minced garlic

1 tablespoon cider vinegar

1 tablespoon water

½ teaspoon dried oregano leaves

½ teaspoon salt

1. Cook the herb seeds in a lightly greased small skillet, stirring frequently, until toasted. Remove from the skillet. Add the ancho chili to the skillet; cook over medium heat until softened, for about 1 minute on each side, turning so the chili does not burn. Remove and discard the stems, veins, and seeds. Chop the chili finely.

2. Combine the pork and all the other ingredients in a small bowl, mixing well. Refrigerate, covered, for at least 4 hours or overnight, so flavors can blend. Shape the mixture into 4 patties; cook in a small lightly greased skillet over medium heat until cooked, for 4 to 5 minutes on each side. Serve immediately.

GYROS PATTIES

These delicious patties combine ground lamb and beef.

4 SERVINGS

8 ounces (227 g) lean ground beef (ask the butcher to make sure it is gluten free)

8 ounces (227 g) ground lamb (see above note about purchasing ground meat)

2 tablespoons chopped onion

2 cloves garlic, minced

½ teaspoon dried oregano leaves

½ teaspoon dill weed

1 teaspoon salt

Gyros Relish (recipe follows)

1. Combine the ground meats, onion, garlic, herbs, and salt; shape into 4 patties. Cook in a large skillet over medium heat to the desired degree of doneness, for about 5 minutes on each side for medium. Serve immediately with the Gyros Relish.

GYROS RELISH

2 CUPS

½ cup (50 g) sliced green onion

½ cup (65 g) seeded, chopped cucumber

½ cup (80 g) seeded, chopped tomato

⅔ cup (158 mL) plain Greek yogurt (Chobani is gluten free)

1 teaspoon dried mint leaves

1 teaspoon dried oregano leaves

1. Combine all the ingredients.

TANDOORI LAMB WITH CUCUMBER RAITA >

Even if you don't have a clay tandoor oven, you can make delicious tandoori-style lamb. All you need is a well-stocked pantry of spices and some Greek yogurt. This recipe is adapted from The Gluten-Free Good Health Cookbook *by Annalise G. Roberts and Dr. Claudia Pillow.*

4–8 SERVINGS

2 cups (474 mL) plain Greek yogurt (Chobani is gluten free), divided

2 tablespoons fresh lemon juice

2 tablespoons peeled and minced fresh ginger

1 tablespoon fresh minced garlic

1 teaspoon salt

1 teaspoon ground coriander

1 teaspoon ground turmeric

½ teaspoon saffron threads, crumbled

½ teaspoon ground cumin

½ teaspoon freshly ground black pepper

½ teaspoon cayenne pepper

2 pounds (908 g) boneless loin of lamb, cut into 2-inch (5-cm) cubes

2 tablespoons olive or coconut oil

¼ cup (4 g) chopped fresh cilantro, for sprinkling

Cucumber Raita (see recipe page 59), for serving

1. To make the marinade, blend 1 cup (237 mL) of the yogurt with the lemon juice, ginger, garlic, salt, coriander, turmeric, saffron threads, cumin, black pepper, and cayenne pepper and process in a food processor until smooth. Transfer to a large bowl and mix in the remaining cup of yogurt.

2. Add the lamb cubes to the marinade; turn to coat. Cover and refrigerate overnight.

3. Preheat the grill to 400°F (200°C). Divide the lamb evenly among 8 long metal skewers. Grill for 10 minutes, turning and basting evenly with the marinade.

4. To finish, baste 1 side of the lamb with the olive oil; cook for 2 minutes. Turn, baste the other side of the lamb with the oil, and cook another 2 minutes.

5. Transfer to a platter, sprinkle with the cilantro, and serve immediately with the Cucumber Raita.

YOUNG LAMB WITH FRESH PEAS

Young lamb, usually served with fresh peas, is featured in U.S. butcher shops in March and April. If you cannot find young lamb, make this dish with regular lamb, but cook it twice as long. This recipe comes from The Puglian Cookbook *by Viktorija Todorovska.*

4 SERVINGS

3 tablespoons (45 mL) extra virgin olive oil

1 large onion, peeled, quartered, and thinly sliced

1½ pounds (681 g) young lamb (shoulder cut), cubed

½ teaspoon salt, plus more, to taste

1 cup (237 mL) dry white wine

1 pound (454 g) frozen peas

Freshly ground black pepper, to taste

½ cup (50 g) grated pecorino cheese (a sheep's milk cheese similar to Parmigiano-Reggiano; grate your own to ensure no wheat products are added to prevent caking)

1. In a large Dutch oven, heat the olive oil over medium heat. Add the onion and cook until softened, for about 5 to 6 minutes.

2. Wash the lamb. Pat it dry with a paper towel and season it with the salt.

3. Add the lamb to the Dutch oven and cook until it is browned on all sides, for about 10 to 12 minutes.

4. Add the wine to the Dutch oven and cook until the alcohol evaporates and the wine reduces by almost half, for about 4 minutes.

5. Reduce the heat to low, cover, and cook for about 1 hour. (The lamb should fall apart when pierced with a fork. If you are using regular lamb, cook it for at least 2 hours over very low heat.)

6. When the lamb is almost done, add the peas and cook for about 5 minutes, until the flavors blend.

7. Season with the salt and pepper to taste. Sprinkle with the pecorino cheese and serve immediately.

FISH AND SEAFOOD

SHRIMP CURRY

Good curry dishes are notorious for requiring a lot of effort. Long lists of ingredients that require chopping, grinding, and roasting often put a dent in our desire to make them at home. But this Indian-style shrimp curry is fragrant and delicious, and it doesn't require hours of prep work in the kitchen. Serve it with basmati rice and some bright green vegetables for a well-balanced meal. This recipe is adapted from The Gluten-Free Good Health Cookbook *by Annalise G. Roberts and Dr. Claudia Pillow.*

4 SERVINGS

1½ pounds (681 g) shrimp, peeled and deveined, with tails removed

2 tablespoons curry powder (I prefer McCormick's spices, because they always list flour on the ingredient label if it's included—check the label carefully to ensure your curry powder is gluten free)

1 teaspoon ground coriander

1 teaspoon ground turmeric

1 tablespoon fresh lemon juice

3 tablespoons (45 mL) organic coconut oil, divided

1 cup (150 g) chopped onion

1 cup (150 g) diced green pepper

1 tablespoon minced peeled fresh ginger

1 tablespoon minced garlic

1 (13.5-ounce [405-mL]) can unsweetened coconut milk

1 cup (237 mL) chicken broth (Pacific Natural Foods chicken broth is gluten free)

½ cup (80 g) canned crushed tomatoes (I use Muir Glen Fire-Roasted Crushed Tomatoes)

2 tablespoons chopped fresh cilantro

Salt and freshly ground black pepper
½ teaspoon cayenne pepper, optional, if your curry is not
   hot enough
Brown basmati rice, for serving

1. Put the shrimp in a small bowl. Mix together the curry powder, ground coriander, and turmeric in another small dish. Take 1 teaspoon of the spice mixture and add it to the shrimp with 1 tablespoon of the oil and the lemon juice. Stir to coat all the shrimp and set aside to marinate for at least 15 minutes.

2. Heat the remaining 2 tablespoons of the oil in a large, heavy skillet over very high heat. Add the shrimp and quickly brown them on both sides, for about 2 minutes total. Remove the shrimp to a small bowl and set aside.

3. Heat the remaining tablespoon of oil in the same skillet over medium-low heat. Add the onion, green pepper, ginger, and garlic; cook until the onion is soft, for about 4 minutes. Add the remaining curry powder, coriander, and turmeric mixture and sauté for about 1 minute. Stir in the coconut milk, broth, crushed tomatoes, and cilantro; bring to a simmer and cover. Cook for 20 minutes over low heat, until the flavors are blended and the sauce has thickened slightly. Remove the cover and cook for another 10 minutes. Season with the salt and pepper, to taste.

4. Add the shrimp and simmer for about 10 minutes (depending on size of shrimp) until the shrimp is hot and cooked through. Add the cayenne pepper, if desired. Serve immediately with the rice.

VARIATION

Chicken Curry—Make recipe as above, but substitute 1½ pounds (681 g) of boneless, skinless chicken cut into 2-inch (5-cm) pieces for the shrimp.

SAUTÉED SEA SCALLOPS WITH CREAMY SHALLOT WINE SAUCE

Scallops are delicious and require relatively little effort to turn them into a special meal. This dish is quick and easy enough for a weeknight supper, but elegant enough to serve if you have guests. We like to pair it with colorful vegetables and a glass of white wine. This recipe is adapted from The Gluten-Free Good Health Cookbook *by Annalise G. Roberts and Dr. Claudia Pillow.*

2 SERVINGS

> ¾ pound (341 g) sea scallops, rinsed and patted dry
> Salt and freshly ground black pepper
> 1 tablespoon butter or olive oil
> ¼ cup (59 mL) white wine
> 2 tablespoons bottled clam juice (Bar Harbor Foods makes an all-natural, no-MSG clam juice)
> 1 tablespoon minced shallots
> 2 tablespoons heavy cream
> 1–2 tablespoons chopped fresh parsley, for sprinkling

1. Season the scallops with salt and pepper, to taste. Heat the butter in a large, heavy skillet over high heat. Add the scallops and cook for 1½ minutes, until just firm and golden in color. Turn and cook the other side another 1½ minutes. Transfer scallops to a small bowl and cover with foil.

2. Add the wine, clam juice, and shallots to the skillet; scrape up the pan drippings. Boil until the liquid is reduced to a little less than ¼ cup (59 mL). Stir in the heavy cream and add the scallops and any juices on the plate. Reduce the heat and cook another minute until the scallops and sauce are heated through. Sprinkle with parlsey and serve immediately.

VARIATION

Sautéed Sea Scallops in Citrus Beurre Sauce—Make recipe as above, but substitute fresh-squeezed lemon or orange juice for the heavy cream and then whisk in a little butter to make a smooth citrus butter sauce. Add chopped fresh herbs, such as basil or thyme.

HALIBUT WITH SOUR CREAM AND POBLANO SAUCE

The picante Sour Cream and Poblano Sauce is also excellent served with shredded chicken breast or lean pork in soft tacos, or over enchiladas.

4 SERVINGS

> 4 halibut steaks (4 ounces [114 g] each)
> 3 tablespoons (45 mL) lime juice
> 1 clove garlic, minced
> Salt and pepper, to taste
> Sour Cream and Poblano Sauce (see recipe on page 62)
> 4 lime wedges

1. Brush the halibut with the combined lime juice and garlic; let stand for 15 minutes. Cook the halibut in a lightly greased large skillet over medium heat until the halibut is tender and flakes with a fork, for 4 to 5 minutes on each side. Sprinkle lightly with the salt and pepper. Serve immediately with the Sour Cream and Poblano Sauce and lime wedges.

TIELLA

This dish is easy comfort food for the summertime. This recipe comes from The Puglian Cookbook *by Viktorija Todorovska.*

4 SERVINGS

1 pound (454 g) mussels

1 cup (237 mL) dry white wine

1 large yellow onion, peeled and thinly sliced

4 large Yukon Gold potatoes, thinly sliced

2 tablespoons extra virgin olive oil

Salt, to taste

10 (about ½ cup [80 g]) grape tomatoes, quartered

1 cup (190 g) uncooked white rice

½ cup (50 g) grated pecorino cheese, for sprinkling (grate your own to ensure no wheat products are added to prevent caking)

½ cup (75 g) toasted gluten-free bread crumbs, for sprinkling (I recommend Glutino and Schar brands)

1. Preheat the oven to 400°F (200°C).

2. Wash the mussels and discard any that are open and will not close when touched. Put the mussels in a medium pan. Add the wine. Cover and cook over medium heat until the mussels are completely open, for about 4 to 5 minutes. Remove the pan from the heat and set aside to cool slightly. Using a fork, take the mussels out of the shells and set them aside. Reserve some of the cooking liquid (a combination of wine and sea water from the mussels).

3. In a medium baking dish, arrange a layer of onions, and then a layer of potato slices. Sprinkle with some olive oil and a little salt, and then layer half the tomatoes. Distribute half the rice as evenly as you can on top and add the mussels. Cover the mussels with more rice, tomatoes, and onions and end with a layer of potatoes. Sprinkle the top layer of potatoes with the remaining olive oil, the pecorino cheese, and the breadcrumbs. Pour some of the cooking liquid from the mussels and add water to come almost ¾ of the way up the sides of the dish. Cook for at least an hour, or until the potatoes are done (they should be tender when pierced with a fork). Serve immediately.

TUNA STEAKS WITH SWEET-SOUR TOMATO-BASIL RELISH >

Spicy tomato relish nicely complements grilled tuna in this easy, elegant recipe.

4 SERVINGS

2 teaspoons olive oil

1 teaspoon minced garlic

1 teaspoon lemon juice

½ teaspoon dried basil leaves

½ teaspoon dried thyme leaves

4 tuna steaks (4 ounces [114 g] each)

Salt and pepper, to taste

Sweet-Sour Tomato-Basil Relish (recipe follows)

1. Combine the olive oil, garlic, lemon juice, and herbs in a small bowl; brush on tuna. Let stand for 15 minutes. Broil the tuna 6 inches (15 cm) from the heat source until the fish is tender and flakes with a fork, for 6 to 8 minutes on each side. Sprinkle lightly with the salt and pepper; serve immediately with the Sweet-Sour Tomato-Basil Relish.

SWEET-SOUR TOMATO-BASIL RELISH

1 CUP

1 large tomato, seeded, cubed
2 tablespoons tomato paste
½ tablespoon water
1½ tablespoons red wine vinegar
1½ tablespoons sugar
1 teaspoon olive oil
¼ teaspoon dried basil leaves
¼ teaspoon dried thyme leaves

1. Sauté the tomato in a lightly greased small skillet until softened, for 3 to 4 minutes; combine with the remaining ingredients.

Note: Make the Sweet-Sour Tomato-Basil Relish before preparing the rest of the recipe.

BAKED FISH WITH POTATOES

This one-pot dish makes a perfect summer meal.

4 fillets flaky white fish (cod, halibut, or other white fish)*
½ cup (119 mL) extra virgin olive oil, divided
1 yellow onion, peeled and chopped
1 clove garlic, peeled and thinly sliced
1 teaspoon red pepper flakes
1 tablespoon salt-packed capers, rinsed
1 cup (237 mL) dry white wine
4 medium potatoes, freshly peeled and cut into small cubes

1.   Preheat the oven to 400°F (200°C).

2.   Wash the fish fillets and pat them dry with a paper towel. Set aside.

3.   In a large pan, heat 3 tablespoons (45 mL) of the olive oil over medium-high heat. Add the onion and cook until soft (but not brown). Add the garlic and red pepper flakes. Toss together and cook for another minute. Add the capers and wine and cook until the wine is reduced by a third.

4.   Brush the bottom of a large baking dish with the remaining olive oil. Distribute the fish and potatoes evenly. Pour the onion and wine mixture over the fish and potatoes, cover, and cook for about 15 minutes, or until the fish is cooked through and the potatoes are soft. Serve immediately.

If the fish fillets are thin and cook faster than the potatoes, transfer them to a heated plate and cover them with foil while you finish cooking the potatoes on the stovetop. If the liquid evaporates completely, add a little warm water.

FLOUNDER EN PAPILLOTE

Traditionally made with a lean white fish, this recipe is also delicious with salmon or tuna.

> 6 flounder, sole or other lean white fish fillets (4 ounces [114 g] each)
> Salt and pepper, to taste
> 1 cup (75 g) sliced mushrooms
> 1 cup (128 g) julienned carrots
> ¼ cup (38 g) finely chopped shallots or onion
> 2 cloves garlic, minced
> ½ teaspoon dried tarragon leaves
> 2 teaspoons butter
> ½ cup (119 mL) dry white wine or water
> ¼ cup (8 g) finely chopped parsley
> 6 lemon wedges

1. Cut six 12-inch (30-cm) squares of parchment paper; fold each in half, and cut each into a large heart shape. Open the hearts and place 1 fish fillet on each; sprinkle lightly with the salt and pepper.

2. Sauté the mushrooms, carrots, shallots, garlic, and tarragon in the butter in a large skillet until the carrots are crisp-tender, for about 5 minutes. Stir in the wine and parsley; season to taste with salt and pepper. Spoon the mixture over the fish. Fold the packets in half, bringing the edges together; crimp the edges tightly to seal. Bake on a jelly roll pan at 425°F (220°C) until the packets puff, for 10 to 12 minutes. Serve immediately with the lemon wedges.

Note: Aluminum foil can be used in place of parchment paper; bake fish for 15 minutes.

RED SNAPPER VERACRUZ

In this famous dish from Veracruz, Mexico, red snapper is baked in a full-flavored tomato sauce with olives and capers. The fish can also be grilled and then topped with the sauce. This recipe comes from 1,001 Best Low-Fat Recipes *by Sue Spitler.*

6 SERVINGS

1 whole red snapper, dressed (about 2 pounds [908 g])
2 tablespoons lime juice
2 cloves garlic, minced
Veracruz Sauce (see recipe on page 67)
6 lime wedges

1. Pierce the surfaces of the fish with a long-tined fork; rub them with the lime juice and garlic. Refrigerate, covered, in a large glass baking dish for 2 hours.

2. Spoon the Veracruz Sauce over the fish. Bake, uncovered, at 400°F (200°C) until the fish is tender and flakes with a fork, for 25 to 35 minutes. Serve immediately with the lime wedges.

PASTA

MACARONI AND CHEESE

This recipe is based on the classic, time-tested recipe loved by kids big and small. It features a simple milk- and potato starch-based roux, enhanced with extra-sharp cheddar cheese—but feel free to make your own additions and changes. Replace some or all of the cheddar with Asiago, Fontina, Swiss, Jarlsberg, goat, or mozzarella cheese, and enhance the flavor with Dijon mustard, red pepper flakes, or other spices. This recipe is adapted from The Gluten-Free Good Health Cookbook *by Annalise G. Roberts and Dr. Claudia Pillow.*

4 SERVINGS

1 pound (454 g) gluten-free elbow macaroni (Tinkyada makes a great brown rice elbow pasta)

3 tablespoons unsalted butter

1 tablespoon potato starch

½ teaspoon dried thyme

½ teaspoon dry mustard

2¼ cup (533 mL) milk (whole is best)

1 (10-ounce [284-g]) box frozen cooked butternut squash, defrosted and puréed

2 cups (about 8 ounces [227 g]) shredded extra-sharp cheddar cheese (shred your own to ensure no wheat products are added to prevent caking)

½ cup grated Parmigiano-Reggiano cheese

Salt and freshly ground black pepper

8 tomato slices and fresh parsley sprigs, for garnish

1. Preheat the oven to 350°F (180°C). Place the rack in the center of the oven. Grease a 1-quart (948-mL) baking dish with cooking spray.

2. Cook the macaroni in a large pot of boiling water until tender. Drain the macaroni; do not rinse it with cold water.

3. While the macaroni is boiling, melt the butter in a medium-sized, heavy saucepan over low heat. Mix the potato starch, thyme, and dry mustard into the melted butter and cook slowly, stirring constantly for 1 minute (the mixture will be bubbly and won't look like a traditional roux). Gradually stir in the milk. Increase the heat to medium and cook, stirring constantly, until the white sauce is smooth, thick, and reaches the boiling point. Whisk in the puréed butternut squash.

4. Reduce the heat and add the shredded cheddar cheese. Stir until the cheese is melted. Spoon the sauce into the macaroni and stir until well combined. Add the salt and pepper, to taste.

5. Spoon the macaroni and cheese into the prepared baking dish. Top with tomato slices and the Parmigiano-Reggiano cheese.

6. Place the baking dish in the center of the oven and bake at 350°F (180°C) for about 20 to 30 minutes, until golden brown and crisp on top. Garnish with fresh parsley and serve immediately.

PASTA WITH CHICKEN AND CREAMY PESTO SAUCE

You can prep the chicken the night before and then come home and have dinner on the table in less than 30 minutes. This recipe is adapted from The Gluten-Free Good Health Cookbook *by Annalise G. Roberts and Dr. Claudia Pillow.*

4 SERVINGS

12 ounces (341 g) gluten-free fusilli (Schar makes tasty gluten-free fusilli)

1 tablespoon olive oil

1 pound (454 g) boneless skinless chicken breasts, thinly sliced

1 tablespoon minced fresh garlic

1 teaspoon dried oregano

½ cup chicken broth

1 cup (134 g) frozen peas, thawed

¾ cup (178 mL) prepared pesto (use good-quality, gluten-free store-bought or homemade pesto)

2 cups chopped fresh spinach

¼ cup (59 mL) heavy cream

½ cup (50 g) grated Parmesan cheese (grate your own to ensure no wheat products are added to prevent caking)

Salt and freshly ground black pepper

1. Cook the pasta according to package directions and drain.

2. Heat the olive oil in a large, heavy skillet over high heat (you can also use a large, heavy 5-quart (4.74-L) saucepan in order to avoid a lot of cleanup). Add the chicken, garlic, and oregano to the pan and sauté until cooked through.

3. Add the broth and scrape up the pan juices. Add the peas, pesto, spinach, cream, and Parmesan cheese. Stir until well combined.

4. Add the pasta and cook until sauce is heated; 1 to 2 minutes. Season with the salt and pepper, to taste. Turn off the heat; cover the pan and allow the pasta to sit for 3 to 4 minutes. Serve immediately.

VARIATION

Pasta with Shrimp and Creamy Pesto Sauce—Make recipe as above, substituting 1½ (681 g) pounds of peeled, deveined shrimp for the chicken. Use bottled clam juice or white wine in place of chicken broth.

ASIAN NOODLES WITH CHICKEN

The fragrant aroma and subtle flavors of this noodle dish will entice you! This recipe is adapted from The Gluten-Free Good Health Cookbook *by Annalise G. Roberts and Dr. Claudia Pillow.*

6 SERVINGS

MARINADE

2 tablespoons hoisin sauce (Premier Japan makes a delicious gluten-free version)

2 tablespoons sake

1 tablespoon soy sauce (I recommend Kikkoman's Gluten-Free Soy Sauce and San-J brands)

1 tablespoon minced garlic

½ teaspoon ginger

1 teaspoon sesame oil

DISH

1½ pounds (681 g) boneless, skinless chicken breasts, thinly sliced

⅔ cup (158 mL) chicken broth (Pacific Natural Foods chicken broth is gluten free)

2 tablespoons creamy peanut butter

2 tablespoons soy sauce (see note above)

2 tablespoons sake

1 tablespoon sesame oil

½ teaspoon Chinese five-spice powder (I prefer McCormick's spices, because they always list flour on the ingredient label if it's included—check the label carefully to ensure your five-spice powder is gluten free)

1 pound (454 g) gluten-free fettuccini (Tinkyada's Brown
    Rice Fettuccini is great)
1 tablespoon organic coconut oil
1 tablespoon minced fresh ginger
2 teaspoons minced garlic
3 ounces (85 g) fresh baby spinach
½ cup (75 g) chopped scallions

1. Make the marinade by combining the hoisin sauce, sake, soy sauce, garlic, ginger, and sesame oil in a medium-sized bowl. Toss the chicken with the marinade until the chicken is well coated. Cover and let sit for 10 minutes or refrigerate for at least 1 hour.

2. Combine the chicken broth, peanut butter, soy sauce, sake, sesame oil, and Chinese five-spice powder in a large measuring cup. Heat the mixture in a small saucepan or in the microwave until hot and set aside.

3. Cook the pasta in a large pot of boiling water until tender. Drain the pasta; do not rinse it with cold water. Return the pasta to the pot.

4. While the pasta is cooking, heat the coconut oil in a large, heavy skillet over medium-high heat (you can also use a large, heavy (5-quart 4.74-L]) saucepan in order to avoid a lot of cleanup). Add the ginger and garlic and cook for 1 minute. Increase the heat to high and add the chicken; sauté until cooked through.

5. Add the cooked pasta and toss until pasta is coated. Add the warm sauce mixture, the baby spinach, and the scallions; toss until well combined. Turn off the heat, cover the skillet, and allow the pasta to sit for 3 to 4 minutes. Serve immediately.

CHICKEN–PASTA SKILLET WITH SUN-DRIED TOMATOES AND OLIVES >

Sun-dried tomatoes and black olives lend a rich, earthy flavor to this colorful dish. This recipe comes from 1,001 Best Low-Fat Recipes by Sue Spitler.

4 SERVINGS

½ cup (75 g) chopped onion

½ cup (75 g) green bell pepper

1 tablespoon olive oil

1 pound (454 g) boneless, skinless chicken breast, cubed (1-inch)

1 large zucchini, cubed

1 can (15½ ounces [434 g]) Italian-seasoned diced tomatoes (I use Muir Glen diced tomatoes with Italian herbs), undrained

1 teaspoon dried marjoram leaves

3 tablespoons (10 g) chopped sun-dried tomatoes

3 tablespoons (25 g) pitted black or Greek olives

Salt and pepper, to taste

4 ounces (114 g) gluten-free rigatoni (Sam Mills Pasta d'Oro brand is gluten free and quite tasty), cooked, warm

1. Sauté the onion and bell pepper in the olive oil in a large skillet until tender, for about 5 minutes; add the chicken and sauté 5 minutes. Stir in the zucchini, tomatoes with liquid, marjoram, sun-dried tomatoes, and olives; heat to boiling. Reduce the heat and simmer, uncovered, until the chicken is cooked and the sauce is thickened, for about 10 minutes; season to taste with the salt and pepper. Serve over the rigatoni immediately.

Note: Begin cooking the rigatoni before preparing the rest of the recipe.

PASTA WITH CREAMY GORGONZOLA AND MUSHROOM SAUCE

This dish pairs the richly pungent flavor of gorgonzola (use a good-quality cheese) with earthy mushrooms to create a satisfying dish with multiple layers of flavor. You can prepare it in 30 minutes or less, so it's perfect for a quick weeknight supper. This recipe is adapted from The Gluten-Free Good Health Cookbook *by Annalise G. Roberts and Dr. Claudia Pillow.*

4 SERVINGS

2 tablespoons olive oil

2 tablespoons minced garlic

¼ cup (38 g) minced shallots

1 pound (454 g) mushrooms, trimmed and sliced

½ cup (119 mL) white wine

½ cup (119 mL) chicken broth (Pacific Natural Foods chicken broth is gluten free)

1 cup (160 g) canned diced tomatoes (I use Muir Glen diced tomatoes), undrained

1 tablespoon dried basil

2 teaspoons dried oregano

1 cup (150 g) crumbled Gorgonzola cheese

2 tablespoons fresh chopped parsley

Salt and freshly ground black pepper

12 ounces (341 g) gluten-free fusilli (Schar makes tasty gluten-free fusilli)

½ cup (50 g) grated Parmesan cheese, for sprinkling

1. Heat the oil in a large, heavy skillet over medium heat. Add the garlic and shallots and cook for 2 minutes, until golden. Add the mushrooms and sauté until they begin to soften, for about 5 minutes. Add the white wine and broth; stir to deglaze the pan. Add the tomatoes, basil, and oregano; bring to a simmer, lower heat, cover, and cook for 3 more minutes (sauce will thicken slightly). Add the Gorgonzola cheese; stir to blend. Season with the salt, pepper, and fresh parsley to taste.

2. While the sauce is simmering, cook the pasta in a large pot of boiling water until tender. Drain the pasta; do not rinse it with cold water. Add the pasta to the skillet with the sauce. Cook over low heat for 2 minutes, so the pasta can absorb some of the sauce. Sprinkle with the Parmesan cheese and serve immediately.

SIDES

BUTTERNUT SQUASH GRATIN

We reduced the fat but not the flavor in this winter classic. This savory gratin features roasted butternut squash, a sweet, nutty vegetable that's high in antioxidants but low in calories. This dish is a wonderful compliment to roasted meat and poultry. To save prep time, buy the peeled and precut fresh squash found in the chilled produce aisle. This recipe is adapted from The Gluten-Free Good Health Cookbook *by Annalise G. Roberts and Dr. Claudia Pillow.*

6 SERVINGS

2 tablespoons olive oil

1 tablespoon pure maple syrup

1 tablespoon minced fresh garlic

½ teaspoon coarse salt

½ teaspoon freshly ground black pepper

⅛ teaspoon cayenne pepper

4 cups butternut squash (about 2 pounds [908 g]), peeled, seeded, and cut into 1-inch (2.5-cm) cubes

1 cup (150 g) peeled and diced sweet onion

½ cup (119 mL) chicken broth (Pacific Natural Foods chicken broth is gluten free)

½ cup (50 g) grated Parmigiano-Reggiano cheese (grate your own to ensure no wheat products are added to prevent caking)

2 tablespoons heavy cream

1 tablespoon chopped fresh sage (or ½ teaspoon dried), divided

½ teaspoon dried thyme

Salt and freshly ground black pepper

1. Preheat the oven to 425°F (220°C). Place the rack in the bottom third of the oven. Line a large baking sheet with foil and grease with oil or cooking spray.

2. In a large mixing bowl, combine the oil, maple syrup, garlic, salt, black pepper, and cayenne pepper. Add the squash and onion and toss until coated with the mixture.

3. Spread the vegetables in a single layer on the prepared baking sheet. Roast, tossing occasionally, until the vegetables are lightly browned and caramelized, for about 25 minutes.

4. While the vegetables are roasting, combine the broth, Parmigiano-Reggiano cheese, cream, half of the sage, and thyme in a medium mixing bowl. Set aside.

5. Remove the vegetables from the oven and toss with the broth mixture in the bowl. Transfer to a medium casserole dish and bake at 400°F (200°C) for 20 minutes. Season with the salt and pepper, to taste. Sprinkle with the remaining sage and serve immediately.

SPINACH AND GOAT CHEESE PIE >

This Spinach and Goat Cheese Pie is a dietitian's delight. Packed with the superfoods spinach and tofu, this dish makes for a perfect side dish with any meal. This recipe is adapted from The Gluten-Free Good Health Cookbook *by Annalise G. Roberts and Dr. Claudia Pillow.*

6 SERVINGS

1 pound (454 g) fresh spinach
2 bunches scallions
1 tablespoon olive oil
2 teaspoons fresh minced garlic
½ teaspoon dried thyme
2 tablespoons chopped fresh basil
2 tablespoons chopped fresh parsley
Salt and freshly ground black pepper
1 cup (250 g) silken tofu
5 ounces (142 g) goat cheese
3 large eggs
1 cup (237 mL) milk
Ground nutmeg, for sprinkling
¼ cup (25 g) shredded Parmesan cheese (shred your own to ensure no wheat products are added to prevent caking)

1. Preheat the oven to 375°F (190°C). Place the rack in the center of the oven. Grease a 9-inch (22.5-cm) pie pan with cooking spray.

2. Remove the stems from the spinach and cut the leaves into large pieces. Wash and spin dry.

3. Trim the roots and most of the greens off the scallions and thinly slice them.

4. Heat the oil in a large fry pan. Add the scallions, garlic, thyme, basil, and parsley, and cook over medium heat for 1 minute.

5. Gradually add the spinach by the handful. Let each batch of spinach soften and wilt before adding the next. Season with the salt and pepper and set aside.

6. In a food processor, purée the tofu. Add the goat cheese and blend until smooth. Then add the eggs and milk. Sprinkle with the nutmeg and season with more salt and pepper, to taste. Blend until well combined.

7. Mix the spinach mixture and custard together in a bowl and spoon into the prepared pan. Sprinkle with the Parmesan cheese. Bake at 375°F (190°C) for 30 minutes, or until set and lightly browned. Allow to rest for 5 minutes before serving.

DAL (CURRIED LENTILS)

Dal is a classic Indian dish that is simple to prepare. Packed with nutrition, it's a staple in most Indian households and is served at many meals. This recipe is adapted from The Gluten-Free Good Health Cookbook *by Annalise G. Roberts and Dr. Claudia Pillow.*

4 SERVINGS

1 tablespoon olive oil or organic coconut oil

1 cup (150 g) minced onion

1 cup (150 g) diced green pepper

1 tablespoon minced fresh garlic

1 tablespoon curry powder (I prefer McCormick's spices, because they always list flour on the ingredient label if it's included—check the label carefully to ensure your curry powder is gluten free)

1 teaspoon fresh grated ginger

1 fresh medium-sized jalapeño pepper, seeded and minced

4 cups (948 mL) chicken broth (Pacific Natural Foods chicken broth is gluten free)

1½ cups (240 g) fresh, or 1 (14.5-ounce [408 g]) can, diced tomatoes, including juice

1 cup (192 g) dried lentils, washed

1 medium-sized sweet potato, freshly peeled and diced

1 teaspoon salt

¼ cup (4 g) finely chopped fresh cilantro, for garnish

Salt and freshly ground black pepper, to taste

1. Heat the oil in a large, heavy (5-quart [4.74-L]) saucepan over medium-high heat. Add the onion, green pepper, garlic, curry powder, ginger, and jalapeño pepper and sauté for about 4 minutes.

2. Add the broth, tomatoes, lentils, sweet potato, and salt and bring to a boil. Reduce the heat to medium; cover loosely and simmer until the lentils are tender, for about 30 minutes.

3. Just before serving, add the cilantro and season with the salt and pepper. Serve immediately.

Note: Lentils can be made ahead of time and stored in the refrigerator for up to 3 days in a tightly sealed container. The leftovers can be stored in the refrigerator for up to 3 days and the freezer for up to 4 weeks in a tightly sealed container. Rewarm over medium-high heat.

SAUTÉED BABY SPINACH WITH GARLIC

Most top-ten superfood lists contain spinach, a leafy green vegetable rich in vitamin A and C, protective phytochemicals, and neutralizing minerals, such as calcium, potassium and zinc. Serve this dish with grilled, roasted, or sautéed meat and seafood, or tossed with brown rice and Parmesan cheese. This recipe is adapted from The Gluten-Free Good Health Cookbook *by Annalise G. Roberts and Dr. Claudia Pillow.*

2–4 SERVINGS

1 tablespoon extra virgin olive oil, divided
2 teaspoons thinly sliced fresh garlic
1 tablespoon raw pine nuts
4 cups (120 g) baby spinach leaves, washed, stemmed, and loosely packed
Salt and freshly ground black pepper

1. Heat ½ tablespoon of the olive oil in a heavy, medium-sized sauté pan over medium heat. Sauté the garlic and pine nuts in the oil for 1 minute.

2. Add the spinach, salt, and pepper to the pan and cook for 90 seconds. Pour the liquid from the pan. Toss with the remaining olive oil. Serve immediately.

CREAMY CORN PUDDING

Creamy Corn Pudding *is a cross between a cornbread and a pudding. This recipe is adapted from* The Gluten-Free Good Health Cookbook *by Annalise G. Roberts and Dr. Claudia Pillow.*

6–8 SERVINGS

½ cup (80 g) white or yellow corn meal

1 tablespoon granulated sugar

1 teaspoon baking soda (Arm & Hammer is gluten free)

½ teaspoon sea salt

½ teaspoon freshly ground black pepper

½ teaspoon dried thyme

1½ cups (356 mL) buttermilk*

½ cup (119 mL) heavy cream

4 large eggs

1 tablespoon unsalted butter, melted

3 cups (450 g) defrosted, frozen white or yellow sweet baby corn kernels

1 tablespoon chopped fresh dill, optional

1. Preheat the oven to 350°F (180°C). Place the rack in the center of the oven. Grease an 11- × 7-inch (27.5- x 17.5-cm) baking dish with cooking spray.

2. Whisk together the corn meal, sugar, baking soda, salt, pepper, and thyme in a large bowl.

3. Pulse the buttermilk, cream, eggs, and butter in a blender or food processor until smooth. Add the corn and dill and pulse a few more times (the mixture should be lumpy, with visible kernels).

4. Whisk the buttermilk mixture into the corn meal mixture. Pour into the prepared baking dish and bake for 30 to 35 minutes, until the edges are golden brown and the center remains slightly jiggly. Transfer to a rack to cool, then serve.

* You can use 6 tablespoons (23 g) powdered buttermilk in 1½ cups (356 mL) water in place of the buttermilk.

MIXED ROASTED VEGETABLES

Good choices for the vegetables include red and yellow peppers, zucchini and yellow squash, baby carrots, halved Brussels sprouts, and asparagus. This recipe is adapted from The Gluten-Free Good Health Cookbook *by Annalise G. Roberts and Dr. Claudia Pillow.*

10 SERVINGS

2 tablespoons olive oil

1 tablespoon pure maple syrup

1 tablespoon minced fresh garlic

½ teaspoon coarse salt

½ teaspoon freshly ground black pepper, or to taste

1 teaspoon herbes de Provence

⅛ teaspoon cayenne pepper, optional

4 cups (600 g) assorted vegetables, cut into approximately 1¼-inch (3.2-cm) chunks

1 cup (150 g) peeled cubed red onion, peeled and cut into approximately 1¼-inch (3.2-cm) chunks

1. Preheat the oven to 425°F (220°C). Place the rack in the bottom third of the oven. Line a large, shallow baking sheet with foil and grease it with oil or cooking spray (the baking sheet should be large enough so the vegetables can be very densely packed in a thick single layer).

2. In a large mixing bowl, combine the oil, maple syrup, garlic (if using), salt, black pepper, herbes de Provence, and cayenne pepper (if using). Add the cut-up vegetables and onion and toss until coated in the mixture.

3. Spread the vegetables on the prepared baking sheet. Roast, tossing occasionally, until the vegetables are lightly browned and caramelized, for about 25 minutes. Serve immediately.

POTATOES AND PEPPERS

You'll be surprised and delighted by the flavor intensity of this simple yet creative combination. This recipe comes from The Puglian Cookbook *by Viktorija Todorovska.*

4 SERVINGS

> 6 medium potatoes
> 2 red bell peppers
> 2 poblano peppers*
> 5 tablespoons (75 mL) extra virgin olive oil
> Salt, to taste
> Freshly ground black pepper, to taste

1. Peel the potatoes and cut them into ½-inch (13-mm) cubes. Boil the cubes in salted water for 10 minutes, or until they are soft but not falling apart. Drain and set aside.

2. Cut the peppers into ¼-inch (6-mm) strips and cut the strips into bite-sized pieces. In a large pan, heat the olive oil over medium-high heat and add the peppers. Cook for 5 minutes, or until they start to soften. Add the potatoes and cook the pepper–potato mixture for another 3 to 5 minutes, or until the potatoes start to brown.

3. Season with the salt and pepper to taste and serve immediately.

* You can use green bell peppers, if you prefer.

MEXICAN-STYLE VEGETABLES AND RICE

Rice combines with vegetables and south-of-the-border flavors.

⅔ cup (100 g) chopped red bell pepper

⅔ cup (100 g) chopped onion

3 cloves garlic, minced

1 jalapeño chili, finely chopped

2 cups (250 g) cubed peeled chayote squash

2 cups (150 g) halved small cremini mushrooms

1 cup (160 g) whole-kernel corn

½ teaspoon dried oregano leaves

½ teaspoon ground cumin

½ teaspoon chili powder (I prefer McCormick's spices, be-cause they always list flour on the ingredient label if it's included—check the label carefully to ensure your chili powder is gluten free)

Salt and pepper, to taste

4 cups cooked white or brown rice

1 cup (237 mL) sour cream (beware low-fat varieties, as they may contain food starches—check labels carefully)

¾ cup (3 ounces [85 g]) shredded Monterey Jack cheese (shred your own to ensure no wheat products are added to prevent caking)

2 green onions, sliced

1. Sauté the bell pepper, onion, garlic, and jalapeño chili in a lightly greased large skillet 5 minutes; add the squash, mushrooms, corn, and herbs. Cook, covered, over medium

heat until the squash and mushrooms are tender, for about 8 minutes, stirring occasionally. Season to taste with the salt and pepper.

2. Spoon half of the rice into a greased 2-quart (1.9-L) casserole. Top with the vegetable mixture and sour cream; spoon the remaining rice on top. Bake, loosely covered, at 300°F (150°C) until hot, for 30 to 40 minutes. Sprinkle with the cheese and bake, uncovered, until the cheese is melted, for 5 to 10 minutes. Sprinkle with the green onions. Serve immediately.

Note: Cook the rice before preparing the rest of the recipe.

SUGAR-GLAZED BRUSSELS SPROUTS AND PEARL ONIONS

Roasted Brussels sprouts are a revelation; this preparation takes things to the next level. The pearl onions can be fresh, frozen, or canned.

4–6 SERVINGS

1 tablespoon butter
¼ cup (50 g) sugar
8 ounces (227 g) halved small Brussels sprouts, roasted until crisp-tender, warm
8 ounces (227 g) pearl onions, roasted until crisp-tender, warm
Salt and white pepper, to taste

1. Heat the butter in a medium skillet until melted; stir in the sugar and cook over medium heat until the mixture is bubbly. Add the vegetables and toss to coat. Season to taste with the salt and white pepper. Serve immediately.

EGG AND BROCCOLI CASSEROLE

A side dish your family will love! This recipe comes from 1,001 Best Low-Fat Recipes *by Sue Spitler.*

4 SERVINGS

2 packages (10 ounces [284 g] each) frozen chopped broccoli, thawed, well drained

4 hard-cooked eggs, thinly sliced

1 cup (237 mL) sour cream (beware low-fat varieties, as they may contain food starches—check labels carefully)

½ cup (119 mL) mayonnaise (both Kraft and Hellman's brands are gluten free)

2 tablespoons white wine vinegar

1½ teaspoons dried tarragon leaves

Paprika, as garnish

1. Arrange the broccoli in a lightly greased 13- x 9-inch (32.5- x 22.5-cm) baking dish; top with the egg slices.

2. Combine the sour cream, mayonnaise, vinegar, and tarragon in a bowl.

3. Transfer the sour cream mixture to a small saucepan and heat the mixture over low heat, stirring until warm, for about 4 minutes. Pour over the broccoli and eggs; sprinkle with the paprika. Bake, uncovered, at 325°F (160°C) for 15 to 20 minutes. Serve immediately.

QUARTET OF ONIONS

Cooked slowly until caramelized, the onion mixture is scented with mint and sage.

6 SERVINGS

2 pounds (908 g) sweet onions, sliced

1 small leek (white part only), thinly sliced

½ cup (75 g) chopped shallots

½ cup (50 g) sliced green onions

½ cup (119 mL) beef, chicken, or vegetable broth or stock (Pacific Natural Foods beef and chicken broths are gluten free)

1–1½ teaspoons dried mint leaves

½ teaspoon dried sage leaves

Salt and white pepper, to taste

1. Sauté the onions, leek, shallots, and green onions in a lightly greased large skillet for 3 to 4 minutes. Stir in the broth and herbs and heat to boiling; reduce the heat and simmer, covered, for 5 minutes. Cook, uncovered, over medium-low heat until the onion mixture is golden, for about 15 minutes. Season to taste with the salt and white pepper. Serve immediately.

DESSERTS

COFFEE PUDDING

This light dessert is easy to make, requires only four ingredients, and has lots of flavor. It is the perfect ending to any meal, and even guests who do not drink coffee enjoy its delicate flavor and smooth texture. This recipe comes from The Puglian Cookbook *by Viktorija Todor-ovska.*

8 SERVINGS

> 2 cups (474 mL) milk
>
> 2 eggs
>
> 4 egg yolks
>
> ¾ cup (150 g) sugar
>
> ½ cup (119 mL) espresso or very strong coffee (be sure the espresso or coffee is gluten free), cooled to room temperature

1. Preheat the oven to 400°F (200°C).

2. In a saucepan, warm the milk over medium-low heat, but do not let it boil.

3. In a clean mixing bowl, combine the eggs, egg yolks, and sugar and beat on high speed for 5 to 6 minutes, or until the mixture is thick and light colored. Add the coffee to the mixture.

4. Temper the warmed milk into the mixture, a little bit at a time, stirring constantly as you go to prevent the eggs from scrambling.

5. Grease 8 individual ramekins. When all the ingredients are combined and the mixture has a uniform texture, divide it among the prepared ramekins.

6. Place the ramekins in a large baking dish. Pour water around the ramekins in the dish until it reaches halfway up the sides of the ramekins.

7. Bake for about 40 minutes, or until the pudding in the ramekins is almost set. The pudding will continue to set as it cools, so do not bake until firm or it will be too dry.

8. Cool to room temperature and then refrigerate for up to 2 days. Serve cold.

CHOCOLATE FUDGE MERINGUES

Better bake several batches—these won't last long!

2 DOZEN COOKIES (1 PER SERVING)

> 3 egg whites
> ½ teaspoon cream of tartar
> ¼ teaspoon salt
> 2 cups (200 g) powdered sugar
> ½ cup (43 g) cocoa powder (I recommend Ghirardelli Unsweetened)
> ½ package (6-ounce [170-g] size) semisweet chocolate morsels, chopped (Enjoy Life makes good gluten-free chocolate)

1. Beat the egg whites, cream of tartar, and salt to soft peaks in a medium bowl. Beat to stiff peaks, adding the sugar gradually. Fold in the cocoa; fold in the chopped chocolate.

2. Drop the mixture by tablespoons onto parchment or aluminum foil-lined baking sheets. Bake at 300°F (150°C) until the cookies feel crisp when touched, for 20 to 25 minutes. Cool on pans on wire racks. Serve immediately.

CHOCOLATE MOUSSE TORTE >

This cake is more complex to make, but filled and frosted with rich chocolate mousse, it will make any occasion special.

12 SERVINGS

> 1 package (16 ounces [454 g]) Bob's Red Mill Gluten-Free Chocolate Cake Mix
> ½ cup (114 g) butter, warmed to room temperature
> 1 cup (237 mL) milk, warmed to room temperature
> 1 tablespoon fresh lemon juice
> 2 large eggs, warmed to room temperature
> ⅓ cup (79 mL) hot water (110°F [43°C])
> 2 teaspoons vanilla extract (McCormick extracts are gluten free)
> Chocolate Mousse (recipe follows)
> ¼ cup (27 g) sliced almonds, toasted

1. Grease the bottoms of three 8- or 9-inch (20- or 22.5-cm) round cake pans and line with parchment paper.

2. In a large bowl using a hand or stand mixer, cream the softened butter until it is smooth. Add the cake mix, milk, lemon juice, and eggs and beat for 30 seconds on low speed until combined. Scrape the sides of the bowl as necessary. Then, beat for 1 minute more on low to medium speed. Add the hot water and vanilla and beat thoroughly for 1 minute more.

3. Spread the batter in the prepared cake pans; bake at 350°F (180°C) until toothpick inserted in center comes out clean, for 15 to 18 minutes. Cool the cakes in pans on wire racks; remove from the pans.

4. Place one of the cake layers, parchment side up, in the bottom of a 9-inch (22.5-cm) springform pan. Discard the parchment. Spread the cake with ⅓ of the Chocolate Mousse;

repeat with the remaining cake layers and Chocolate Mousse. Sprinkle the top of the cake with almonds. Refrigerate for 8 hours or overnight.

5. Loosen the cake from the side of the pan with a sharp knife; remove the side of the pan and place the cake on serving plate. Serve immediately.

CHOCOLATE MOUSSE

4 CUPS

1 envelope (¼ ounce [7 g]) unflavored gelatin (Knox's brand is gluten free)

¼ cup (59 mL) cold water

1 cup (200 g) sugar, divided

½ cup (43 g) cocoa powder (I recommend Ghirardelli Unsweetened)

1¼ cups (296 mL) 2% milk

2 egg yolks

4 ounces (114 g) semisweet chocolate, finely chopped (Enjoy Life makes good gluten-free chocolate)

2 egg whites

⅛ teaspoon cream of tartar

1. Sprinkle the gelatin over the cold water in a small saucepan; let stand 3 to 4 minutes. Heat over low heat until the gelatin is dissolved, stirring constantly.

2. Mix ½ cup (100 g) of the sugar and the cocoa in a small saucepan; whisk in the milk. Heat to boiling over medium-high heat; reduce the heat and simmer briskly, whisking constantly, until thickened, for 3 to 4 minutes. Whisk about ½ of the milk mixture into the egg yolks; next, whisk the egg yolk mixture into the milk mixture in the saucepan. Cook over low heat for 1 to 2 minutes, whisking constantly. Remove from the heat; add the

gelatin mixture and the chocolate, whisking until the chocolate is melted. Refrigerate until cool, but not set, for about 20 minutes.

3. Beat the egg whites, the remaining ½ cup (100 g) sugar, and the cream of tartar until foamy in a medium bowl; place the bowl over a pan of simmering water and beat at medium speed until the egg whites reach 160°F (71°C) on a candy thermometer. Remove from the heat and beat at high speed until very thick and cool, for about 5 minutes. Mix ¼ of the egg whites into the chocolate mixture; fold the chocolate mixture into the remaining egg whites until completely blended.

CHERRY PECAN MERINGUES

A colorful holiday offering—use red cherries for February sweethearts.

3½ DOZEN COOKIES (1 PER SERVING)

>   3 egg whites
>   ⅛ teaspoon cream of tartar
>   ¼ teaspoon salt
>   1 cup (200 g) sugar
>   ¼ cup (27 g) finely chopped toasted pecans
>   ¾ cup (113 g) finely chopped gluten-free maraschino
>   cherries (Walmart's Great Value brand is gluten free)

1. Beat the egg whites, cream of tartar, and salt to soft peaks in a large bowl. Beat to stiff peaks, adding the sugar gradually. Fold in the pecans and cherries.

2. Drop the mixture by tablespoons onto parchment or aluminum foil-lined baking sheets. Bake at 300°F (150°C) until the cookies begin to brown and feel crisp when touched, for 15 to 20 minutes. Cool on wire racks. Serve immediately.

Orange Meringues—Make the cookies as above, adding ½ teaspoon orange extract (McCormick extracts are gluten free), substituting ⅓ cup (36 g) almonds for the pecans, and eliminating the cherries.

HAZELNUT MACAROONS

Use your favorite nuts in these moist and crunchy macaroons.

1½ DOZEN COOKIES (1 PER SERVING)

> 4 egg whites
> ⅛ teaspoon cream of tartar
> ¼ teaspoon salt
> 1 cup (200 g) sugar
> 1 cup (93 g) flaked coconut
> ¼ cup (36 g) finely chopped hazelnuts or pecans

1. Beat the egg whites, cream of tartar, and salt to soft peaks in a medium bowl. Beat to stiff peaks, adding the sugar gradually. Fold in the coconut and hazelnuts.

2. Drop the mixture by tablespoons onto parchment or aluminum foil-lined baking sheets. Bake at 300°F (150°C) until the cookies begin to brown and feel crisp when touched, for 20 to 25 minutes. Cool on wire racks. Serve immediately.

VARIATION

Island Dreams—Make the cookies as above, adding ½ teaspoon pineapple extract (McCormick extracts are gluten free), reducing the coconut to ½ cup (47 g), and substituting macadamia nuts for the hazelnuts. Fold in ½ cup chopped dried pineapple or mango; bake as above.

CHOCOLATE INDULGENCE BROWNIES

Dark chocolate, moist and gooey—a brownie that's too good to be true!

2 DOZEN BROWNIES (1 PER SERVING)

3 eggs

¾ cup (169 g) packed light brown sugar

2 teaspoons vanilla

2 cups (200 g) gluten-free chocolate cookie crumbs (try Nana's No Gluten Chocolate Crunch Cookies)

3 tablespoons (16 g) cocoa powder (I recommend Ghirardelli Unsweetened)

¼ teaspoon salt

⅔ cup (98 g) chopped dates

½ cup (90 g) semisweet chocolate morsels (Enjoy Life makes good gluten-free chocolate)

1. Beat the eggs, brown sugar, and vanilla in a large bowl until thick, for about 2 minutes. Fold in the cookie crumbs, cocoa, and salt; fold in the dates and chocolate morsels.

2. Spread the batter evenly in a greased 11 x 7-inch (27.5 x 17.5-cm) baking pan. Bake at 300°F (150°C) until the top springs back when touched and the brownies begin to pull away from the sides of the pan, for about 40 minutes. Cool on a wire rack. Serve warm or store chilled in the refrigerator.

PUTTING ON THE RITZ BARS

Never have rice cereal treats been quite so glamorous! This recipe comes from 1,001 Best Low-Fat Recipes *by Sue Spitler.*

2½ DOZEN BARS (1 PER SERVING)

> 1 package (10 ounces [284 g]) marshmallows (the Kraft version doesn't contain modified food starch, so it's a good choice)
> 4 tablespoons (57 g) butter
> 3 cups (84 g) rice cereal (Rice Krispies® has a whole-grain, gluten-free version made with brown rice)
> ½ cup (47 g) flaked coconut
> 1 cup (112 g) dried cranberries or raisins
> 1 cup (112 g) chopped dried mixed fruit
> ½–¾ cup (57–86 g) coarsely chopped walnuts
> 2 ounces (57 g) semisweet baking chocolate, melted and warm (Enjoy Life makes good gluten-free chocolate)

1. Heat the marshmallows and butter in a large saucepan over low heat until melted, stirring frequently. Stir in the remaining ingredients, except the chocolate, mixing well.

2. Spoon the mixture into a greased 15 x 10-inch (37.5 x 25-cm) jelly roll pan, pressing into an even layer. Refrigerate for 1 hour.

3. Drizzle the top with the warm chocolate; refrigerate until set, for about 15 minutes. Cut into bars. Serve immediately.

CARAMEL FLAN

Unbelievably delicate and fine in texture, this flan is one you'll serve over and over again.

8 SERVINGS

⅔ cup (134 g) sugar, divided
4 cups (948 mL) 2% milk
5 eggs, lightly beaten
2 teaspoons vanilla extract (McCormick extracts are gluten free)

1. Heat ⅓ cup (67 g) of the sugar in a small skillet over medi-um-high heat until the sugar melts and turns golden, stirring occasionally (watch carefully, as the sugar can burn easily!). Quickly pour the syrup into the bottom of a 2-quart (1.9-L) soufflé dish or casserole and tilt the bottom to spread the caramel. Set aside to cool.

2. Heat the milk and the remaining ⅓ cup (67 g) sugar until steaming and just beginning to bubble at the edges. Whisk into the eggs; add the vanilla. Strain into the soufflé dish over the caramel.

3. Place the soufflé dish in a roasting pan on the middle oven rack. Cover the soufflé dish with a lid or aluminum foil. Pour 2 inches (5 cm) of hot water into the roasting pan. Bake at 350°F (180°C) for 1 hour or until a sharp knife inserted half-way between the center and edge of the custard comes out clean. Remove the soufflé dish from the roasting pan and cool on a wire rack. Refrigerate for 8 hours or overnight.

4. To unmold, loosen the edge of the custard with a sharp knife. Place a rimmed serving dish over the soufflé dish and invert. Serve immediately.

Pumpkin Flan—Make the flan as above, reducing the milk to 2 cups (474 mL) and mixing 1 cup (245 g) canned pumpkin purée (check the label to make sure it doesn't contain modified food starch or any other hidden sources of gluten) and 1 teaspoon cinnamon into the milk mixture.

BANANAS FOSTER

A real taste of New Orleans!

4 SERVINGS

> ¼ cup (56 g) packed light brown sugar
> 1½ teaspoons corn starch
> ½ cup (119 mL) water
> 1 tablespoon rum or ½ teaspoon rum extract (McCormick extracts are gluten free)
> 1 teaspoon vanilla extract (McCormick extracts are gluten free)
> 2 medium bananas, sliced
> ¼ cup (25 g) toasted pecan halves
> 1⅓ cups (316 mL) vanilla ice cream (Breyers and Dreyers are gluten free)

1. Mix the brown sugar and corn starch in a small saucepan; stir in the water and heat to boiling. Boil, stirring, until thickened, for about 1 minute.

2. Stir in the rum and vanilla; add the bananas and simmer until hot, for 1 to 2 minutes. Stir in the pecans; serve immediately warm over the ice cream.

HERBED CUSTARD BRULÉE

Scented with herbs, this delicate custard is topped with a sprinkling of caramelized brown sugar.

6 SERVINGS

3 cups (711 mL) 2% milk

2 tablespoons minced fresh or ½ teaspoon dried basil leaves

2 tablespoons minced fresh or ½ teaspoon dried cilantro leaves

2 tablespoons minced fresh or ½ teaspoon dried tarragon leaves

5 eggs

½ cup (119 mL) granulated sugar

¼ cup (56 g) packed light brown sugar

1. Heat the milk and herbs to boiling in a medium saucepan. Remove from the heat, cover, and let stand 10 minutes. Strain; discard the herbs.

2. Beat the eggs and granulated sugar in a medium bowl until thick and lemon-colored, for about 5 minutes. Gradually whisk the milk mixture into the eggs; strain the mixture and pour it into eight 6-ounce (240-mL) custard cups.

3. Place the custard cups in a roasting pan on the center oven rack; pour 2 inches of hot water into the pan. Bake, uncovered, at 350°F (180°C) for 20 minutes or until a knife inserted halfway between the center and edge of the custards comes out clean. Remove the cups from roasting pan and cool on a wire rack. Refrigerate until chilled, for 2 to 4 hours.

4. Press the brown sugar through a strainer evenly over the chilled custards. Place on a baking sheet and broil, 4 inches (10 cm) from the heat source, until the sugar is melted and caramelized, for 2 to 3 minutes. Serve immediately.

VARIATIONS

Maple Crème Brulée—Make the recipe as above, reducing the milk to 2 cups (474 mL), the granulated sugar to ¼ cup (50 g), and omitting the herbs. Boil 1 cup (237 mL) pure maple syrup until it is reduced to ⅓ cup (79 mL); add to the milk in Step 1.

Coconut Crème Brulée—Make the recipe as above, substituting ½ cup (47 g) toasted flaked coconut for the herbs in Step 1 and adding 1 teaspoon vanilla and ¾ teaspoon coconut extract (Mc-Cormick extracts are gluten free) to the strained milk mixture. Complete recipe as above.

Coffee Crème Brulée—Make the recipe as above, omitting the herbs. Heat 1 tablespoon instant espresso or coffee powder (make sure it is a gluten-free variety, such as Caffe D'Vita) with the milk in Step 1, stirring until dissolved. Increase the granulated sugar to ⅔ cup (134 g), and add 2 tablespoons coffee liqueur (Kahlua is gluten free) in Step 2.

BAKED BANANA SOUFFLÉS

For perfect flavor and texture, select bananas that are ripe and soft, but not overripe. The soufflé can also be baked in a 1-quart soufflé dish. Bake at 450°F (230°C) for 10 minutes, then at 425°F (220°C) for about 10 additional minutes.

6 SERVINGS

> 2 ripe bananas, peeled
> 2 teaspoons lemon juice
> 1 teaspoon vanilla extract (McCormick extracts are
>   gluten free)
> ¼ cup (50 g) sugar, divided
> ¼ teaspoon ground nutmeg
> 2 egg yolks
> 4 egg whites
> ½ teaspoon cream of tartar

1. Process the bananas, lemon juice, vanilla, 1 tablespoon of the sugar, and the nutmeg in a food processor or blender until smooth. Add the egg yolks, one at a time, blending until smooth.

2. Beat the egg whites and cream of tartar in a medium bowl to soft peaks; gradually beat in the remaining 3 tablespoons (38 g) of sugar, beating to stiff peaks. Fold in the banana mixture. Spoon into 6 lightly greased 1-cup (237-mL) soufflé dishes or custard cups. Place the dishes on a baking sheet.

3. Bake, uncovered, at 450°F (230°C) for 7 minutes; reduce the heat to 425°F (220°C) and bake until the soufflés are lightly browned and a sharp knife inserted near the centers comes out clean, for about 7 minutes. Remove from the oven; serve immediately.

DOUBLE CHOCOLATE SOUFFLÉ >

This fabulously rich chocolate soufflé is accented by White Chocolate Sauce. Melt the white chocolate very carefully, as it can easily become grainy.

10 SERVINGS

¼ cup (59 mL) simple syrup*

¼ cup (59 mL) light corn syrup (Karo is gluten free)

3 ounces (85 g) semisweet chocolate, grated and melted (Enjoy Life makes good gluten-free chocolate)

2 tablespoons cocoa powder (I recommend Ghirardelli Unsweetened)

2 teaspoons instant espresso powder (Caffe D'Vita is gluten free) or instant coffee granules (Taster's Choice is gluten free)

1 egg yolk

5 egg whites

¼ cup (50 g) granulated sugar plus more for sprinkling

1 tablespoon powdered sugar

White Chocolate Sauce (recipe follows)

1. Mix the applesauce, chocolate, cocoa, espresso, and egg yolk until well blended.

2. Beat the egg whites in a large bowl to soft peaks; beat to stiff peaks, adding the granulated sugar gradually. Fold ¼ of the egg white mixture into the chocolate mixture. Fold the

* Making simple syrup is just that—simple. To make 1½ cups (356 mL) of simple syrup (much more than you'll need for this recipe), combine 1 cup of sugar and 1 cup (237 mL) of water in a medium saucepan. Bring the mixture to a boil, stirring constantly, until all the sugar has dissolved. Cool the syrup before using it in the recipe. Store the rest of the syrup in your refrigerator—it's useful in cocktails and other recipes and should last about a month.

chocolate mixture into the egg white mixture. Pour into a 2-quart (1.90-L) soufflé dish that has been lightly greased and sprinkled with sugar.

3. Place the soufflé dish in a square baking pan on the center rack of the oven. Pour 2 inches (5 cm) of boiling water into the pan. Bake at 350°F (180°C) until puffed and set, for about 55 minutes. Sprinkle with the powdered sugar. Serve immediately with the White Chocolate Sauce.

WHITE CHOCOLATE SAUCE

½ CUP (119 ML)

2 tablespoons 2% milk

3 ounces (85 g) white chocolate, chopped (Ghirardelli's white chocolate baking bars are gluten free, but the company's classic white chocolate chips may contain gluten)

1 tablespoon brewed coffee or coffee liqueur (optional) (Kahlua is gluten free)

1. Heat the milk over low heat in a small saucepan to simmering; add the white chocolate and whisk over very low heat until melted. Remove from the heat; stir in the coffee or liqueur.

COEUR À LA CRÈME

This dessert is perfect for Valentine's Day. The traditional Coeur à la Crème (Cream Heart) mold is porcelain, with holes in the bottom to drain the excess liquid from the cheeses. With this recipe, any 5-cup mold can be used.

6 SERVINGS

> 2 envelopes unflavored gelatin (Knox's brand is gluten free)
> ¾ cup (178 mL) 2% milk
> 2 cups (474 mL) 4% cottage cheese (Friendship, Creamland Dairies, and Breakstone's are gluten free)
> 1 package (8 ounces [227 g]) Neufchâtel or cream cheese
> 3 tablespoons (38 g) sugar
> 1 teaspoon vanilla extract (McCormick extracts are gluten free)
> Whole strawberries, as garnish
> 3 cups (450 g) sliced strawberries or fresh raspberries

1. Sprinkle the gelatin over the milk in a small saucepan; let stand for 1 minute. Stir over low heat to just simmering.

2. Process the cottage cheese in a food processor until smooth. Add the cream cheese, sugar, vanilla, and gelatin mixture and process until smooth. Pour the cheese mixture into a lightly greased 5-cup (1.2-L) heart-shaped mold or cake pan. Cover; refrigerate until firm, for 3 to 4 hours.

3. Dip the mold briefly in warm water and loosen the edge of the cheese mixture with a sharp knife; unmold onto a serving platter. Garnish with the whole strawberries; serve with the sliced strawberries.

INDEX

Also from Agate Surrey

ANNALISE G. ROBERTS
Gluten-Free
Baking Classics
FOR THE Bread Machine

"The only bread machine and recipe book you will ever need to make the best gluten-free breads on earth. Five Stars."

—The Best Bread Makers blog

ISBN 978-1-57284-104-8 · $14.95

Available at booksellers everywhere

SURREY
BOOKS

Also from Agate Surrey

ABOUT THE SERIES

Each of the books in the *101* series features delicious, diverse, and accessible recipes—101 of them, to be exact. Scattered throughout each book are beautiful full-color photographs to show you just what the dish should look like. The *101* series books also feature a simple, contemporary design that's as practical as it is elegant, with measures calculated in both traditional and metric quantities.

ABOUT THE EDITOR

Perrin Davis is co-editor of Surrey's *101* series. She lives with her family in suburban Chicago.